How a Film Theory Got Lost and Other Mysteries in Cultural Studies

How a Film Theory Got Lost

and Other Mysteries in Cultural Studies

Robert B. Ray

Indiana University Press

BLOOMINGTON AND INDIANAPOLIS

This book is a publication of

Indiana University Press
601 North Morton Street
Bloomington, IN 47404-3797 USA

http://www.indiana.edu/~iupress

Telephone orders   800-842-6796
Fax orders   812-855-7931
Orders by e-mail   iuporder@indiana.edu

© 2001 by Robert B. Ray

*The paper used in this publication meets the minimum
requirements of American National Standard for Information
Sciences—Permanence of Paper for Printed Library Materials,
ANSI Z39.48-1984.*

MANUFACTURED IN THE UNITED STATES OF AMERICA

Library of Congress Cataloging-in-Publication Data

Ray, Robert B. (Robert Beverley), date
    How a film theory got lost and other mysteries in cultural studies / Robert B. Ray.
        p.   cm.
    Includes bibliographical references and index.
    ISBN 0-253-33851-4 (cl : alk. paper) — ISBN 0-253-21438-6 (pa : alk. paper)
        1. Motion pictures—Philosophy. 2. Film criticism.   I. Title.

PN1995 .R39 2001
791.43′01—dc21
                                                                          00-061399

1 2 3 4 5   06 05 04 03 02 01

To my brothers, Charles Barham Ray and Russell Beverley Ray, Jr.

CONTENTS

F O R E W O R D

by James Naremore

Most readers of this volume are probably familiar with Robert B. Ray's first book, *A Certain Tendency of the Hollywood Cinema: 1930–1980*, an engaging and ambitious commentary on the ideology of classic Hollywood containing important readings of *Casablanca*, *It's a Wonderful Life*, *The Godfather*, *Taxi Driver*, and many other legendary films. That book was written at a moment in the history of academic film studies when the liberal-humanist theory of André Bazin and the iconoclastic auteurism of *Cahiers du cinéma* had been almost entirely displaced by radical critiques of Hollywood's "apparatus." In the spirit of the times, Ray made brilliant use of both structuralist and post-structuralist ideas: like Jim Kitses and Charles Eckert, he argued that Hollywood narrative (which, he noted, is always similar to the plot of a western) functions in the same fashion as myth, magically reconciling society's irreconcilable contradictions; and like Noel Burch, he demonstrated that Hollywood's illusionist style, with its emphasis on continuity editing and individual subjectivity, operates to conceal the sources of enunciation, thereby making a conservative mythology seem natural, real, and true.

A Certain Tendency remains the best one-volume discussion of Hollywood in the sound era, and in my own view its arguments about the ideological significance of American popular fiction are as relevant as ever. And yet, even though I doubt that Ray would want to retract much of what he said, he no longer writes about the media in the same way. His later publications, which include *The Avant-Garde Finds Andy Hardy* and the series of essays collected here, are oriented toward the cultural studies movement, which usually examines film within the larger context of modernity and postmodernity. They also represent his attempt to jump the tracks of ordinary academic discourse and achieve a mode of written communication that will be commensurate with the photographic and electronic age. Because of this last aim, any sympathetic introduction to his recent work is almost obliged to describe him by adopting his own ludic techniques, which include lists, recipes, montages, manifestos, puns, and experiments in free association. I shall therefore try to explain him in the form of a brief list entitled (à la Godard) "Five or Six Things I Know about Robert Ray":

1. Ray has identified a "certain tendency" not only in movies but also in American media studies. The carefully bounded academic institution or "field" that deals with movies and TV takes its methods from history and literary criticism (with a bit of sociology and anthropology thrown in to bolster its scientific credentials) and is always rationalist in disposition, suspicious of ideas derived from unconventional means. Like institutional Hollywood, it creates highly predictable works, employing hermeneutic protocols that inhibit free association and encourage a sense of interpretive closure. Also like Hollywood, it controls the inherent "drift" or indeterminacy of photographic images by subordinating them to a narrative logic and a linguistic sign system.

2. If there is a connection between form and ideology, and if the philosopher Walter Ong, whom Ray quotes at several junctures, is correct to say that new modes of communication create different ways of thinking, then the academics who study the contemporary media need to catch up with their technological environment, creating new intellectual paradigms and new forms of discovery. Together with his University of Florida colleague Gregory Ulmer, Ray believes that the best way to achieve these ends is to learn from contemporary pop culture and from the postmodern philosophy of Jacques Derrida, Roland Barthes, and Michel Foucault. "What if academics were to write essays the way Paul Simon [or Public Enemy] now writes songs?" he asks at one point. Equally important, he and Ulmer contend that academics need to borrow strategies from the historical avant-garde. Where Ray in particular is concerned, French surrealism is an especially important model to follow, chiefly because it developed out of what he describes as "the photographic sensibility."

3. In "Snapshots," an intriguing essay collected in this volume, Ray points out that photography was originally used to document the urban masses and to

control the modern threat of invisibility and anonymity. But in a dialectical movement of "revenge," the photographic image produced an excess of information, creating what Roland Barthes has called a "third meaning." This meaning was generated by sheer automatism and could never be purely contained by a linguistic or narrative context. The surrealists cherished its subversive power and tried to unleash its anarchic potential through a discontinuous, fragmented style of filmmaking and a distracted technique of film viewing. Hollywood, on the other hand, harnessed its "eros" to the service of glamour and enchantment.

4. All of Ray's recent work is indebted to surrealism, but this does not mean that his essays are disassociated and oneiric in the manner of André Breton's *Nadja*. His writing is lucid, based on solid research into film history, and he often sounds like a charismatic trial lawyer laying out the evidence of a case. In one sense he is influenced less by surrealist artists than by the great cultural critics who have used surrealist methods—most notably by Walter Benjamin's *Arcades Project* and Roland Barthes's *S/Z*. A far less Freudian writer than the original surrealists (though he has important things to say in defense of the fetish), he wants to blur the distinction between art and criticism, and he sometimes aspires to a "readymade" or a montage of quotations. In the tradition of the avant-garde, he favors detournement, remotivation, and the recycling of texts and styles. He devalues hermeneutics in favor of what Gregory Ulmer calls "heuristics," and throughout his essays he makes us aware of the aleatory, the contingent, the accidental. Repeatedly, he argues on behalf of a nonliterary style of communication that would involve a "relaxation of the explanatory drive" and a free-ranging, associative technique that can find mysterious links between apparently disparate phenomena. Because he frequently employs this technique himself, his essays are a good deal more fun than the average academic paper— they move quickly and easily, leaping over disciplinary boundaries, establishing connections between far-flung events, and sending out unpredictable flashes of illumination.

5. Ray wants to move our attention from the authorized, presumably autonomous work of art to the process of textuality; in his own words, he wants us to think of the art object as a "site, a crossroads traversed by communicative highways continually rerouted by external, extratextual circumstances." He describes his approach as "postmodern," and most readers would probably agree. For my own part, however, I feel a need to quibble with his terminology. My problem is not so much that postmodernism's advocates keep claiming Mallarmé, Apollinaire, Joyce, and Borges as their exemplars, but that they inevitably caricature their modernist "Other." In most instances,

modernism and postmodernism are two sides of the same coin, opposed not so much to each other as to a certain kind of realism. (That is why in *S/Z* Barthes opposed the "readerly" Balzac to the "writerly" moderns.) Thus when Ray criticizes modernism in his wonderfully provocative essay "The Bordwell Regime and the Stakes of Knowledge," he seems to me to be talking less about the actual projects of *Ulysses, The Waste Land,* or even *Citizen Kane* than about academic high modernism of the 1950s and after. At any rate, he demonstrates that cultural meaning is unstable, always dependent on its context, and constantly subject to appropriation and remotivation.

6. The original surrealists were fond of games such as "the exquisite corpse" or "the irrational expansion of a film scene," which suspended conscious mental activity in favor of automatism. As critics and teachers, they were also fond of posing irrelevant questions about texts. (Unlike the Anglo-American New Critics, they thought it was not only OK but also interesting to ask how many children had Lady Macbeth.) To play the surrealist games well, however, it helps if you are a gifted artist or writer. Ray fits this description perfectly. In addition to being a fine scholar and teacher, he is a talented musician, a poet of some accomplishment, and one of the most skillful essayists in film studies. Despite the fact that he sometimes discusses recondite materials, and despite the fact that he challenges some of our assumptions about language and representation, his argument always has uncommon wit, flair, and ease. Such an effect is achieved only through hard work, and it is the sign of a writer who respects both his medium and his audience. To slightly revise a famous statement by Mallarmé, whom Ray quotes at one point, the best theoretical writing consists not merely of ideas but of skillfully employed *words.* Ray takes this axiom seriously, and the form of his essays is intended as proof of their general argument. He wants his audience to experience the joy of learning, and one of the most evident traits of his essays is that they enact their argument, giving us an intellectual and verbal pleasure to match the aural and visual pleasure of their subject matter. This is why the essays that follow will appeal to a wide audience of intellectuals and will outlast most academic publication.

ACKNOWLEDGMENTS

I am especially grateful to Joan Catapano and Michael Lundell at Indiana University Press for sponsoring this book, and to Jane Lyle for seeing it through the publication process. I appreciated, too, the careful copyediting, and witty queries, of Stephanie G'Schwind. A sabbatical awarded by the University of Florida enabled me to complete this book. My thanks also go to the journal and book editors who first commissioned many of these essays. Their sources are as follows:

1. "How a Film Theory Got Lost" appeared as "Impressionism, Surrealism, and Film Theory: Path Dependence, or How a Tradition in Film Theory Gets Lost," in *The Oxford Guide to Film Studies*, ed. John Hill and Pamela Church Gibson (New York: Oxford University Press, 1998). Reprinted by permission of Oxford University Press.

2. "Snapshots: The Beginnings of Photography" appeared in Robert B. Ray, *The Avant-Garde Finds Andy Hardy* (Cambridge, Mass.: Harvard University Press, 1995). Reprinted by permission of the President and Fellows of Harvard College.

3. "The Bordwell Regime and the Stakes of Knowledge" appeared in *Strategies* 1 (Fall 1988).

4. "Tracking" appeared in *The South Atlantic Quarterly* 90, no. 4 (Fall 1991), ed. Anthony DeCurtis.

5. "How to Start an Avant-Garde" appeared in *The Antioch Review* 52, no.

1 (1994). Copyright © 1994 by the Antioch Review, Inc. Reprinted by permission of the editors.

6. "How to Teach Cultural Studies" was first published in *Studies in the Literary Imagination* 31, no. 3 (Spring 1989). Copyright © 1998, Department of English, Georgia State University. Reproduced by permission.

7. "The Mystery of Edward Hopper" appeared as a film flyer for *Edward Hopper and the American Cinema,* a film series accompanying a Hopper retrospective at the Whitney Museum of American Art: *New American Film and Video Series* no. 75 (New York: Whitney Museum of American Art, 1995).

8. "The Riddle of Elvis-the-Actor" was written for this book.

9. "The Two Cities and the Archive: Notes on Godard" was written for this book.

10. "Film and Literature" appeared as "The Field of 'Literature and Film,'" in *Film Adaptation,* ed. James Naremore (New Brunswick, N.J.: Rutgers University Press, 2000).

How a Film Theory Got Lost and Other Mysteries in Cultural Studies

How a Film Theory Got Lost

1. Film Theory's Two Traditions

In the fall of 1938, when the movies were only forty years old, Walter Benjamin received a rejection letter. Inspired by Louis Aragon's Surrealist narrative *Le Paysan de Paris* (1927) and by Soviet experiments with cinematic montage, Benjamin had conceived what has come to be known as *The Arcades Project*, a history of nineteenth-century Paris constructed primarily from found material—texts, documents, images—whose juxtaposition would reveal the buried origins of modern life. Benjamin had been receiving financial support from Frankfurt's Institute for Social Research, relocated in New York, and he had submitted three chapters of a book on Baudelaire, designed as a prologue to the more experimental work ahead. But speaking for the institute, Benjamin's friend Theodor Adorno said no. "Your study," Adorno wrote, in the now famous passage, "is located at the crossroads of magic and positivism. That spot is bewitched. Only theory could break the spell."[1]

Although Adorno came to regret this decision, his formulation of it defines the history of film theory. For what could be a more exact definition of the cinema than "the crossroads of magic and positivism"? Or a more succinct definition of film theory's traditional project than to "break the spell"?

As a technologically based, capital-intensive medium, the movies quickly developed into an industry keenly attracted by positivism's applications: the Taylorist-Fordist models of rationalized production. Indeed, as Thomas Schatz has described, the Hollywood studios set the tone by explicitly imitating the organizational system developed in large-scale manufacturing.[2] Mass production, standardized designs, concentration of the whole production cycle in a single place, a radical division of labor, the routinizing of workers' tasks, even the after-hours surveillance of employees—all of these Fordist practices became Hollywood's own. Thus, at the peak of its early-1930s power, MGM could produce one feature film per week, a quota enabled by its standardized genres, enormous physical plant, strict definition of roles, and a star system whose performers remained as alienated from their tasks as any factory worker. And to guarantee this system's reliability, L. B. Mayer kept watch on his personnel's every move.

And yet, for all its commitment to the positivism that Taylor and Ford had perfected, Hollywood was not making Model Ts. That ascetic vehicle, a triumph of functionalism, had succeeded by avoiding any traces of the irrational decoration that Ford portrayed as wasteful, inefficient, and "feminine." Strikingly, however, the Model T's decline (Ford abandoned the car in 1927) coincided with Hollywood's ascendancy, as Ford's increasingly successful rival, General Motors' Alfred Sloan, began to demonstrate the enormous, seductive power of style.[3] In doing so, Sloan was deriving an explicit business practice from the crucial discovery intuited by Hollywood's moguls: the movies succeeded commercially to the extent that they enchanted.

Hence the inevitable question: could enchantment be mass-produced? The movies' most influential form, Hollywood cinema (what Noël Burch calls the Institutional Mode of Representation),[4] arose as an attempt to address this problem. The calculus has always been a delicate one: the temptations of rationalization on the one hand, the requirements of seduction on the other. As a result, any commercial filmmaking represents a site of negotiation between these conflicting positions. "The cinema," Jean-Luc Godard once told Colin MacCabe, "is all money,"[5] but at any moment it can also become, as Godard once wrote of Renoir's La Nuit du carrefour (1932), "the air of confusion . . . the smell of rain and of fields bathed in mist."[6]

Developed as the means for balancing filmmaking's competing demands,

Hollywood's protocols became the norm of cinema. Increasingly, film history has suggested that the key figure in their development was less D. W. Griffith than MGM's Irving Thalberg. Far more than the independent Griffith, Thalberg spent his days negotiating between L. B. Mayer's insistence on thrift and the popular audience's demand for glamour. In effect, he occupied Adorno's crossroads, embracing both positivism and magic. Working at the origins of the cinema's dominant mode, a rationalist longing to be enthralled by his own productions, Thalberg in fact embodied the two tendencies of all subsequent film theory.

Film history's conceptual neatness depends on its dual provenance in those great opposites, Lumière and Méliès, documentary and fiction. "Cinema," Godard famously summed up, "is spectacle—Méliès—and research—Lumière," adding (impatient with the forced choice) that "I have always wanted, basically, to do research in the form of a spectacle."[7] Inevitably, film theory took longer to appear, but after the First World War it quickly developed into two analogous positions, only one of which was attached so neatly to a single name.

That name, of course, was Eisenstein. With his insistence that filmmaking as an art depended on repudiating the camera's automatic recording capacity, Eisenstein aligned himself not only with Méliès but also with pictoralism, the movement that sought to legitimize photography by disguising its images as paintings. Eisenstein avoided that retrograde move while nevertheless sharing its fundamental premise: that a medium's aesthetic value is a direct function of its ability to transform the reality serving as its raw material. For Eisenstein, the means of such transformation was montage, the ideal tool for deriving significance (chiefly political) from the real details swarming in his footage.

As his theoretical essays appeared in the 1920s, Eisenstein assumed the role simultaneously perfected by T. S. Eliot—the artist-critic whose writings create the taste by which his own aesthetic practice is judged. Eisenstein's sensational films enhanced the prestige of his theoretical positions, which quickly triumphed over the alternative proposed by the French Impressionists and Surrealists. If Eisenstein saw the cinema as a means of argument, the French regarded it as the vehicle of revelation, and the knowledge revealed was not always expressible in words. "Explanations here are out of place," Louis Delluc wrote about the "phenomenon" of Sessue Hayakawa's screen presence, an example of what the Impressionists called *photogénie*. "I wish there to be no words," Jean Epstein declared, refusing to translate the concept that he posited as "the purest expression of cinema."[8]

The concept of *photogénie,* especially in the Surrealists' hands, emphasized precisely what Eisenstein wished to escape: the cinema's automatism. "For the first time," André Bazin would later elaborate, "an image of the world is formed automatically, without the creative invention of man."[9] Moreover, for reasons that the French could not define, the camera rendered some otherwise ordinary objects, landscapes, and even people luminous and spellbinding. Lumière's simple, mesmerizing films had proved that fact. Eisenstein anticipated Brecht's proposition that "less than ever does the mere reflection of reality reveal anything about reality . . . something must in fact be built up, something artificial, posed."[10] The French who followed Lumière, however, insisted that just turning on the camera would do the trick: in René Clair's words, "There is no detail of reality which is not immediately extended here [the cinema] into the domain of the wondrous."[11] And in his first published essay, Louis Aragon suggested that this effect did not result from "art" films alone:

All our emotion exists for those dear old American adventure films that speak of daily life and manage to raise to a dramatic level a banknote on which our attention is riveted, a table with a revolver on it, a bottle that on occasion becomes a weapon, a handkerchief that reveals a crime, a typewriter that's the horizon of a desk, the terrible unfolding telegraphic tape with magic ciphers that enrich or ruin bankers.[12]

This response seems, in retrospect, an acute description of the way movies are often experienced—as intermittent intensities (a face, a landscape, the fall of light across a room) that break free from the sometimes indifferent narratives that contain them. Why, then, was the Impressionist-Surrealist approach so rapidly eclipsed by Eisenstein's? First, its emphasis on fragmentation poorly suited the rapidly consolidating commercial cinema, whose hard-earned basis lay precisely in its continuity system. Both the Impressionists and the Surrealists, in fact, often regarded narrative as an obstacle to be overcome. ("The telephone rings," Epstein complained, pointing to the event that so often initiates a plot. "All is lost."[13]) Surrealist film-watching tactics, for example, were designed to reassert the autonomy and ambiguity of images: think, for example, of Man Ray's habit of watching the screen through his fingers, spread to isolate certain parts of the screen. Lyrical, contemplative, enraptured by the camera's automatism, the Impressionist attitude derived more from Lumière's way of working than from that of Méliès's. The latter's commitment to fiction, and his willingness to construct a narrative world out of discontinuous fragments, proved the premise of all subsequent commercial filmmaking, including Eisenstein's, which quickly attracted the attention of the Hollywood studios. (Samuel Goldwyn: "I've seen your film *Potemkin* and admire it very much. What I would like is for you to do something of the same kind, but a little cheaper, for Ronald Colman.") Although Méliès had begun as a magician, the filmmaking tradition he inspired lent itself readily to the Taylorist procedures adopted by the American moguls. It was Lumière who had discovered the cinema's alchemy.

Second, by insisting that film's essence lay beyond words, the *photogénie* movement left even its would-be followers with nowhere to go. As Paul Willemen has suggested, "mysticism was indeed the swamp in which most of the theoretical statements of the Impressionists eventually drowned."[14] By contrast, Eisenstein had a thoroughly linguistic view of filmmaking, with shots amounting to ideograms, which, when artfully combined, could communicate the equivalent of sentences. As the hedonistic 1920s yielded to the intensely politicized 1930s, Eisenstein's propositions seemed a far more useful way of thinking about the cinema.

In fact, however, while *photogénie*'s elusiveness caused the term to disappear gradually from film theory, other people were thinking about it—people such as Irving Thalberg. Having perfected its continuity system by the mid-1920s, the Hollywood studios turned to the great remaining problem. MGM's constant screen tests; its commitment to having the best cameramen, costume designers, and lighting technicians; its regular resort to previews—these practices indicated Thalberg's obsessive quest for the photogenic actor, location, or moment. MGM's preeminence during this period suggests that Thalberg achieved, however intuitively, what the Impressionist theoreticians did not: a formula for *photogénie*.

Current film theory has often discredited the Impressionist-Surrealist approach by pointing to *photogénie*'s obvious connection to fetishism. Aragon's own explanation of the cinematic marvelous, amounting to a precise definition of the fetishist's gaze, confirms this diagnosis: "To endow with a poetic value that which does not yet possess it, to willfully restrict the field of vision so as to intensify expression: these are two properties that help make cinematic *décor* the adequate expression of modern beauty."[15]

In its history, fetishism has appeared most prominently as knowledge's opposite, as a means of false consciousness and disavowal. Marx, for example, argued that the "fetishism of commodities" encourages us to ignore the exploitative social relations that such objects simultaneously embody and conceal. The commodity is a "hieroglyph," all right, but not one meant to be read. It substitutes the lure of things for a curiosity about their production. Similarly, Freud posited fetishism as the result of an investigation's arrest. Fearing the sight of the mother's genitals, misunderstood as "castrated," the male infant stops at another place (a foot, an ankle, a skirt's hem), investing this replacement with libidinal energy but denying the sexual difference his gaze has discovered.

What film theory discredited, however, Hollywood skillfully employed. In fact, the development of classical narrative cinema finds its exact parallel in the etymology of the word "fetish." As William Pietz has shown,[16] the problem of fetishism first arose in a specific historical context: the trading conducted by Portuguese merchants along the coast of West Africa in the sixteenth and seventeenth centuries. Renaissance businessmen, the Portuguese were looking for straightforward economic transactions. Almost immediately, they were frustrated by what Pietz evocatively calls "the mystery of value." For the Africans, material objects could embody—"simultaneously and sequentially—religious, commercial, aesthetic, and sexual" worth, and the balance among these categories seemed, at least to the Europeans, a matter of caprice.[17] Especially troubling was the Africans' unpredictable estimate of not only their own objects, but also those of the European traders, which the merchants themselves regarded as "trifles."

Like the Portuguese traders, commercial filmmakers began naïvely by proposing an uncomplicated deal: a story in exchange for the price of a ticket. But they were quickly surprised by their viewers' fascination with individual players. For a brief moment, the industry resisted this unintended consequence of the movies, this admiration for actors that seemed an "overestimation of value," a fetishism. Preserving the players' anonymity, after all, had minimized their power and kept them cheap. Inevitably, however, Hollywood came to recognize this fetishism as a means of making money, and the star system deliberately set out to encourage it. In fact, although continuity cinema's insistence on story often reduced the immediate attraction of its components ("while an image could be beautiful," one cameraman recalls, "it wasn't to be so beautiful as to draw attention to itself"), inadvertently, as the Impressionists and Surrealists saw, the movies glamorized everything: faces, clothes, furniture, trains. A dining car's starched white linen (in *North by Northwest*), a woman's voice (Margaret Sullavan's in *Three Comrades*), a cigarette lighter (*The Maltese Falcon*)—even the most ordinary objects could become, as Sam Spade put it in a rare literary allusion, "the stuff that dreams are made of."[18]

It is hard to know whether this effect was always intended. Constant economic pressures, the conversion to sound, and the absolute preeminence of narrative all encouraged Hollywood's tendency toward Fordist procedures and laconic filmmaking. The American cinema's functionalism, in other words, abetted the rationalist theoretical tradition descending from Eisenstein. In this context, Thalberg's more complicated approach seems especially significant. For despite MGM's production quotas, strict regimentation, and highly developed division of labor, Thalberg often encouraged, or at least allowed, moments of the kind so admired by the Impressionists and Surrealists. In 1932's *Grand Hotel*, for example, whose production he closely supervised, the camera cuts suddenly to an unmotivated overhead shot of Garbo in her balle-

1. Garbo in *Grand Hotel*

rina costume, alone for the first time, opening like a flower as she settles wearily to the floor. The narrative idles, enabling this instance of *photogénie* to unfold because, as Thalberg knew, the movie would be the better for it. The plot could wait.

2. Path Dependence

One of the most decisive moments in the history of film theory occurred during a span of twelve months from 1952 to early 1953. Having emerged from the Second World War alive, but with the teaching career for which he had trained foreclosed to him because of a stammer and poor health,[19] André Bazin confirmed his commitment to film criticism with "The Evolution of the Language of Cinema" and "The Virtues and Limitations of Montage," essays in which, for the first time, someone suggested that the two most prestigious schools of filmmaking (Soviet montage and German Expressionism) were wrong.[20] The movies' possibilities, Bazin insisted, were more radical than those ways of working had suggested.

Bazin, of course, is famous for arguing that film's true destiny is the objective representation of reality. "The guiding myth . . . inspiring the invention of cinema," he had argued a few years earlier, "is the accomplishment of that which dominated in a more or less vague fashion all the techniques of the mechanical reproduction of reality in the nineteenth century, from photography to the phonograph, namely an integral realism, a recreation of the world in its own image, an image unburdened by the freedom of interpretation of the artist or the irreversibility of time."[21] The Soviets and Germans, according to Bazin, had betrayed this sacred purpose by "putting their faith in the image" instead of in reality, convulsing the camera's objectivity with abstracting montages and grotesque *mise-en-scène.*[22]

Since about 1970, this position has been represented as fantastically naïve, another version of Western culture's longing for what philosopher Jacques Derrida calls "unmediated presence." In a passage often singled out for critique, Bazin had apparently earned this attack by praising *The Bicycle Thief* (1948) as "one of the first examples of pure cinema": "No more actors, no more story, no more sets, which is to say that in the perfect aesthetic illusion of reality there is no more cinema."[23] In fact, however, behind Bazin's realist aesthetic lay an intuition about the cinema's most profoundly radical aspect: its automatism. With photography, Bazin kept insisting, an absolutely accurate representation of the world could be produced, for the first time in history, by accident. This miraculous revelatory power made the Soviet or Expressionist imposition of subjective meanings seem a kind of misguided vanity.

This argument, of course, amounted to a displacement of Bazin's unrequited religious impulse. But it also involved a revival of the Impressionists' *photogénie* and the Surrealists' automatism. In his own proposed dictionary entry, André Breton had designated this feature of modern technology as Surrealism's defining activity:

Surrealism, n. Psychic automatism in its pure state, by which one proposes to express—verbally, by means of the written word, or in any other manner—the actual functioning of thought. Dictated by thought, in the absence of any control by reason, exempt from any aesthetic or moral concern.[24]

Breton had also made explicit the metaphoric connection between technology and the Surrealists' favorite game, describing automatic writing as "a true photography of thought."[25] For the Impressionists, *photogénie* was untranslatable but intentional, the product of particularly talented filmmakers. For the Surrealists, on the other hand, it was often accidental, and thus capable of appearing anywhere. Man Ray made the point provocatively: "The worst films I've ever seen, the ones that send me to sleep, contain ten or fifteen marvelous minutes. The best films I've ever seen only contain ten or fifteen valid minutes."[26]

Like the Surrealists, Bazin could occasionally find what he valued in forgettable movies. He devoted, for example, a page-long footnote in "The Virtues and Limitations of Montage" to what he called "an otherwise mediocre English film," *Where No Vultures Fly* (1951), praising a single moment that abandoned a "tricky" and "banal montage" to show parents, child, and a stalking lioness "all in the same full shot."[27] In general, however, Bazin preferred to associate his cinematic ideal with a particular set of strategies deliberately employed by an elect group of filmmakers. Jean Renoir, Vittorio De Sica, F. W.

Murnau, Robert Flaherty, William Wyler, and Orson Welles were great because in relying on long takes and deep focus, they had modestly permitted reality to speak for itself.

With this argument, Bazin was retreating from his thought's most radical implication, his sense of the fundamental difference between previous representational technologies and the new "random generators"[28] like the camera. In the hands of his followers, the *Cahiers* critics, Bazin's attitude toward intentionality became even more ambivalent. *La politique des auteurs* seemed to renounce altogether the Surrealist faith in chance, celebrating even Bazin's beloved "reality" less than the filmmaking geniuses who could consciously summon its charms. But at the heart of the *Cahiers* position lay a privileged term that evoked both *photogénie*'s ineffability and the Surrealists' "objective chance."

That term was *"mise-en-scène."* As the *Cahiers* critics used it, *mise-en-scène* quickly left behind its conventional meaning ("setting") to become a sacred word, shared by friends who could invoke it knowing the others would understand. At first, it appeared to be simply another version of *photogénie,* a way of talking again about the untranslatable "essence of the cinema." Hence, Jacques Rivette on Otto Preminger's *Angel Face:* "What tempts [Preminger] if not . . . the rendering audible of particular chords unheard and rare, in which the inexplicable beauty of the modulation suddenly justifies the ensemble of the phrase? This is probably the definition of something precious . . . its enigma—the door to something beyond intellect, opening out onto the unknown. Such are the contingencies of *mise-en-scène.*"[29] *Auteurism*'s basic problem, however, involved just this kind of attribution. More than even most theoretical groups, the *Cahiers* critics had a sense of themselves as a visionary, well-educated, sensitive elect. As long as they were associating the delights of *mise-en-scène* with filmmakers like Jean Renoir, they could continue to insist on the conscious aspect of a director's decisions. Renoir, after all, was aesthetically well-bred, politically liberal, and personally sympathetic. But the *auteurist* position increasingly prompted them to celebrate directors who had often made bad films, and who sometimes seemed neither particularly smart nor especially nice. Directors, for example, such as Otto Preminger. Faced with this situation, the *Cahiers* writers revised their praise, directing it less at individual filmmakers than at the medium itself. Thus, the *Cahiers*'s American operative Andrew Sarris could explicitly modulate *la politique des auteurs* into a revival of Surrealism's praise of automatism:

For me, *mise-en-scène* is not merely the gap between what we see and feel on the screen and what we can express in words, but is also the gap between the intention of the director and his effect upon the spectator. . . . To read all sorts of poignant profundities in Preminger's inscrutable urbanity would seem to be the last word in idiocy, and yet there are moments in his films when the evidence on the screen is inconsistent with one's deepest instincts about the director as a man. It is during those moments that one feels the magical powers of *mise-en-scène* to get more out of a picture than is put there by a director.[30]

The roots of this move lay in Bazin's tacit renewal of the Impressionist-Surrealist branch of film theory. This achievement usually goes unnoticed, since Bazin, after all, remains famous for so many other things: his championing of realism and the Italian post-war cinema, his editorship of the *Cahiers,* his spiritual fathering of the *Nouvelle Vague.* Nevertheless, Bazin's ability to reroute film theory, at least temporarily, amounted to a rare instance of a discipline escaping from what economic historians call *path dependence.*[31]

Path dependence developed as a way of explaining why the free market's invisible hand does not always choose the best products. Beta and Macintosh lose to inferior alternatives, while a clumsy arrangement of keyboard symbols (known as QWERTY, for the first six letters on a typewriter's upper left) becomes the international standard. Although an initial choice often occurs for reasons whose triviality eventually becomes evident (momentary production convenience, fleeting cost advantages), that decision establishes a path dependence almost impossible to break. Superior keyboard layouts have repeatedly been designed, but with every typist in the world using QWERTY, they have no chance.

Bazin recognized that film theory was especially prone to path dependence. The vagaries of film preservation, the industry's encouragement of amnesia (before television, only a handful of films were regularly and widely revived), the small size of the intellectual film community—these factors all encouraged theoretical consensus. While the Impressionist and Surrealist films, with a few exceptions, had disappeared from sight, Eisenstein's had remained in wide circulation, serving as advertisements for his position. (And vice versa: Jean-Marie Straub once observed that everyone thinks that Eisenstein was great at editing because he had so many *theories* about it.[32]) As a result, Eisenstein's rationalist, critical branch of film theory had triumphed, establishing a path dependence that Bazin challenged with all his energy.

Bazin attacked on two fronts. First, he challenged the Eisenstein tradition's basic equation of art with anti-realism. Second, he encouraged, without practicing himself, a different kind of film criticism: the lyrical, discontinuous, epigrammatic flashes of subjectivity-cum-analysis that appeared in the *Cahiers du cinéma.* A few now-famous examples from Godard suggest this form's tone:

There was theatre (Griffith), poetry (Murnau), painting (Rossellini), dance (Eisenstein), music (Renoir). Henceforth there is cinema. And the cinema is Nicholas Ray.

Never before have the characters in a film [Ray's *Bitter Victory* (1957)] seemed so close and yet so far away. Faced by the deserted streets of Benghazi or the sand-dunes, we suddenly think for the space of a second of something else—the snack-bars on the *Champs-Elysées,* a girl one liked, everything and anything, lies, the treachery of women, the shallowness, of men, playing the slot-machines. . . .

How can one talk of such a film? What is the point of saying that the meeting between Richard Burton and Ruth Roman while Curt Jurgens watches is edited with fantastic *brio?* Maybe this was a scene during which we had closed our eyes.[33]

In many cases, this different critical strategy evolved into filmmaking itself, with Godard again providing the explanation:

As a critic, I thought of myself as a filmmaker. Today, I still think of myself as a critic, and in a sense I am, more than before. Instead of writing criticism, I make a film, but the critical dimension is subsumed. I think of myself as an essayist, producing essays in novel form or novels in essay form: only instead of writing, I film them.[34]

The film theory sponsored by Bazin would receive its best explanation only after its own moment had passed. Writing in 1973, Roland Barthes proclaimed, "Let the commentary be itself a text. . . . There are no more critics, only writers."[35]

Bazin's moment lasted only fifteen years. The events of May 1968 discredited both his ideas and the critical practice he had fostered, stimulating different questions about the cinema's relationship to ideology and power. The post-1968 period coincided with the development of academic film study, and although *auteurism* briefly persisted as a way of doing film criticism (aided by its explicit analogy to literary authorship), its apolitical concern with aesthetics suddenly seemed reactionary. Comolli and Narboni's 1969 *Cahiers* editorial "Cinema/Ideology/Criticism"[36] represented the transition, an attempt to preserve the old *auteurist* heroes (Ford, Capra, et al.) in terms of the new political criteria. But as film studies spread through the universities, it organized itself around a theoretical approach having more to do with Eisenstein than with Bazin.

That approach has come to be known as "semiotic," using that term as a shorthand way of summarizing the structuralist, ideological, psychoanalytic, and gender theory it encompassed. Committed largely to a species of critique defined by the Frankfurt School, this paradigm accomplished wonderful things, above all alerting us to popular culture's complicities with the most destructive, enslaving, and ignoble myths. It taught us to see the implications of those invisible operations that Brecht had called "the apparatus," the relation, for example, between Hollywood's continuity system, apparently only a set of filmmaking protocols, and a worldview eager to conceal the necessity of choice.[37]

These gains did not come free of charge. The Impressionist-Surrealist half of film theory fell into obscurity, banished for its political irrelevance. Indeed, "impressionistic" became one of the new paradigm's most frequently evoked pejoratives, designating a theoretical position that was either "untheorized" or too interested in the wrong questions. The wrong questions, however, frequently turned on the reasons why people went to the movies in the first place, the problem so vital to the Impressionists. In 1921, Jean Epstein had announced that "The cinema is essentially supernatural. Everything is transformed. . . . The universe is on edge. The philosopher's light. The atmosphere is heavy with love. I am looking."[38] In the new dispensation, occasional film theorist Fredric Jameson would acknowledge that the appeal of beautiful and exciting storytelling is precisely the problem: "Nothing can be more satisfying to a Marxist teacher," he admitted, "than to 'break' this fascination for students."[39] Also rendered suspect was formally experimental criticism, deemed irresponsible by rationalist critique. The *Cahiers*-inspired *auteurist* essay receded, as did the New Wave film, that hybrid of research and spectacle—Lumière and Méliès.

Twenty-five years ago, Roland Barthes recognized what was happening to criticism. The semiotic paradigm that he himself had done so much to establish, "it too," Barthes lamented, "has become in some sort mythical: any student can and does denounce the bourgeois or petit-bourgeois character of such and such a form (of life, of thought, of consumption). In other words, a mythological doxa has been created: denunciation, demystification (or demythification), has itself become discourse, stock of phrases, catechistic declaration."[40] The problem, Barthes wrote four years later, is "Where to go next?"[41] In the next decade, the most important debates in film theory will turn on the extreme path-dependence Barthes saw constraining the humanities. At stake will be our disciplines' ability to produce information, defined by information theory as a function of unpredictability. (The more predictable the message, the less information it contains.[42] Film studies, in particular, should ask these questions: (1) Can the rational, politically sensitive Eisenstein tradition reunite with the Impressionist-Surrealist interest in *photogénie* and automatism? Can film theory, in other words, imitate filmmaking and recognize that, at its best, the cinema requires, as Thalberg understood, a subtle mixture of logical structure and untranslatable allure? (2) Can film theory revive the *Cahiers-Nouvelle Vague* experiment, learning to write differently, to stage its research in the form of a spectacle? American theorist Gregory Ulmer has specified that this new writing practice would provide a complement to critique. It will not be hermeneutics, the science of interpretation, but will look to photography, the cinema, television, and the computer as the source of ideas about invention. It is called *heuretics*.[43]

A heuretic film studies might begin where *photogénie*, third meanings, and fetishism intersect: with the cinematic detail whose insistent appeal eludes precise explanation. Barthes maintained that third meanings, while resisting obvious connotations, compel "an interrogative reading." In doing so, he was implicitly suggesting how Impressionist reverie could prompt an active research method resembling the Surrealists' "Irrational Enlargement," a game in which players generate chains of associations from a given object.[44] Here are the instructions for such a project: Select a detail from a movie, one that interests you without your knowing why. Follow this detail wherever it leads and report your findings.

Here is an example of what this Impressionist-Surrealist model might produce. Studying MGM's Andy Hardy movies, I was struck by the occasional presence of a Yale pennant on Andy's wall. Following Barthes's "instructions," I "interrogated" this object, producing the following response:

In Andy's bedroom, only two pennants appear: Carvel High and Yale. In the 1930s, when the best of the Hardy films were made, Yale's two most famous alumni were probably Cole Porter (author of the college's football cheer) and Rudy Vallee (popularizer of "The Whiffenpoof Song"). *Andy Hardy's Private Secretary* (1941) gives Porter's "I've Got My Eyes on You" to Kathryn Grayson, who uses it to satisfy Andy's request (and the audience's) for something besides opera. But with his urbanity, dandyism, aristocratic wit, and cosmopolitan allusiveness, Porter is the Hardy series's antonym. Vallee's deportment, on the other hand—a studied juvenescence deployed to conceal a prima donna's ego—seems more like Rooney's own. In bursts of manic exuberance, Andy is given to expressions of self-satisfaction addressed to his bedroom mirror, pep talks descended from Franklin's *Autobiography*. Although the Hardy films unquestioningly accept Poor Richard's vulgarized legacy (chambers of commerce, boosterism, faith in "Progress"), those values will eventually be satirized by even popular culture, especially in 1961's *How to Succeed in Business without Really Trying*, whose hero-on-the-make serenades his own mirror image with the show's hit, "I Believe in You." Making a Mickey Rooney–style comeback, that play's costar, in the part of corporation president J. B. Biggley, was Rudy Vallee.

And yet, with the series making no other mention of it, the choice of the Yale pennant seems particularly arbitrary. Andy, after all, eventually follows in his father's footsteps to Wainwright College, whose plentiful coeds, accessible teachers, and intimate size represent the Ivy League's opposite. Obvious answers, of course, present themselves: Yale as the best known college name, Yale as a signifier of "class." Then why not Harvard or Princeton? If we acknowledge instead another logic (more visual, more cinematic), we might begin to see Yale as an unusually valuable design—bold (the rare capital Y), concise (the shortest college name), memorable (the locks), available for multiple rhymes (including "hale," the inevitable companion of Hardy's near-homonym "hearty"). From this perspective, the Yale pennant signals a relaxation of filmmaking's referential drive, a turn toward the possibilities inherent in shapes, movements, and sounds. In the Hardy series, Yale suggests the cinema's revision of Mallarmé's famous warning to Degas—movies are not made with words, but with images.[45]

2 Snapshots: The Beginnings of Photography

In the late twentieth century, the ubiquity of photography, especially as a document of certain events, has engendered a longing for both its earlier invention and its more extensive presence. We now wish that photography had always existed and that it had been everywhere. What did certain things look like exactly—the expression on Napoleon's face when Moscow first appeared in the distance? the hands of John Wilkes Booth, in hiding, waiting to assassinate Lincoln? the clothes worn by the Council of Trent? Einstein at the moment of completing the Theory of Relativity? More and more, to have not seen becomes equated with Walter Benjamin's definition of *catastrophe:* "to have missed the opportunity."[1]

Nothing encourages this desire for photographic evidence more than the cinema, which, as Jean-Luc Godard has pointed out, always provides, at the very least, a documentary record of a particular moment's objects and people:

2. Harlow in *Red Dust*

as Godard said about his own *Breathless,* "This film is really a documentary on Jean Seberg and Jean-Paul Belmondo."[2] Thus, if we want to know, for example, what Jean Harlow looked like less than a week after her husband, Paul Bern, was found dead in an apparent suicide, we have only to look at a scene from *Red Dust,* shot on her first day back on the set but edited without the closeups that her haggard appearance made unusable.[3] In fact, Hollywood's version of the cinema, what Noël Burch calls the Institutional Mode of Representation,[4] dramatically stimulates the desire, and even the expectation, to observe everything. By implicitly guaranteeing its audience the ideal vantage point for every narratively relevant event, by visually underlining (with, for example, closeups, rack focusing, and camera movements) every important detail or expression, Hollywood's "invisible style" accustoms us to expect photographic accompaniment for everything that might prove significant.

What about the origins of photography itself, its first moments of invention and use? What would they look like on film? What if, by the sheerest chance, we came across a roll of film containing a photographic record of just those things but produced by a camera whose strange mechanism, an alternative to the lineage of our own, has been lost? Searching for a manual, we fall upon these remarks, which will serve as our instructions: "The past has left behind in literary texts images of itself that are comparable to the images which light imprints on a photosensitive plate. Only the future possesses developers active enough to bring these plates out perfectly."[5] Think, then, of each of the following sections as a snapshot of photography's beginnings, developed in terms of our current interests in texts, their ways of producing meaning, and their relation to what we still call "the real."

I.

In the course of his first random stroll through the boule-
vards and the rue de la Paix, Lucien, like all new-comers to
Paris, took more stock of things than of persons. In Paris,
it is first of all the general pattern that commands attention. The luxury of the shops, the height of the buildings,
the busy to-and-fro of carriages, the ever-present contrast
between extreme luxury and extreme indigence, all these
things are particularly striking. Abashed at the sight of this
alien crowd, the imaginative young man felt as if he himself
was enormously diminished.
            —Honoré de Balzac, Lost Illusions

In the twenty-year period from 1830 to 1850, when the hero of Balzac's *Lost
Illusions* arrives in Paris, many of the features associated with "modern life"
begin to appear for the first time: the metropolis, the daily newspaper, mass
transit, the department store, the democratization of culture. In particular, between 1839 and 1842, three things happen: the word *photography* begins to
be used for the first time in English and German,[6] the *physiologies* become the
first best-selling mass-market paperback books, and Poe invents the detective
story. What connects these three developments?

Dana Brand has argued that modern urban life provoked a crisis of "legibility."[7] As newcomers swarmed into the cities, abandoning their native sur-
roundings that time, size, and tradition had rendered effortlessly comprehen-
sible, anonymity became a condition that almost everyone experienced at
some point during the day—in a remote *quartier,* visited for the first time on
business; on an unknown street, turned down by mistake; in a neighborhood
encountered in the morning rather than the afternoon. Inevitably, this dislocation encouraged crime: "It is almost impossible," Benjamin quotes a Parisian
undercover policeman observing, "to maintain good behaviour in a thickly
populated area where an individual is, so to speak, unknown to all others and
thus does not have to blush in front of anyone."[8] In December 1840, Edgar
Allan Poe explicitly connected crime to the illegibility of the anonymous "man
of the crowd," who like "a certain German book . . . does not permit itself to
be read."[9] That man, for whom Poe's literate narrator can discover no com-
forting classification, stands for "the type and the genius of deep crime."[10]

Thus, a proposition: what cannot be read threatens. The first sites of this
new anxiety were Paris and London, vast metropolises where people could disappear without a trace, where (as in Balzac and Dickens, the great chroniclers
of the potential anonymity haunting all urban identities) credentials, antecedents, and even names became suspect. The first clue connecting this experience to photography is geographical: photography was invented almost simultaneously in France (by Niepce and Daguerre) and in England (by Fox Talbot).

2.

The Count de Lanty was small, ugly, and pock-marked: dark
as a Spaniard, dull as a banker.
                                            —Balzac, Sarrasine

In *S/Z*, an analysis not only of Balzac's Sarrasine but of all popular narratives, Barthes repeatedly asks, how does Balzac know that Spaniards are dark, bankers dull? Barthes answers by proposing that the realistic novel works precisely to ensure that the source for such a sentence "cannot be discerned": "Who is speaking? Is it Sarrasine? the narrator? the author? Balzac-the-author? Balzac-the-man? romanticism? bourgeoisie? universal wisdom? The intersection of these origins creates the writing."[11] Barthes labels these formulaic expressions ("dark as a Spaniard," "dull as a banker") "cultural codes" or "reference codes" and traces their origin not to reality itself, but to representations of it:

> The cultural codes, from which the Sarrisinean text has drawn so many references, will also be extinguished (or at least will emigrate to other texts; there is no lack of hosts). . . . In fact, these citations are extracted from a body of knowledge, from an anonymous Book whose best model is doubtless the School Manual. (*S/Z*, 205)

For Barthes, of course, the term "School Manual" functions as a metaphor for the imaginary collation of common sense, received ideas, and cultural stereotypes on which the Reference Code relies. In fact, however, something very like actual manuals, guides to the urban scene, did achieve enormous success in Paris between 1840 and 1842: the *physiologies*. The first mass-market, paperback, pocket-sized books, the *physiologies* proved enormously appealing to readers wanting an immediately legible account, however misleadingly simplified, of the cosmopolitan crowd. Roughly 120 different *physiologies* appeared during these three years, each offering what historian Richard Sieburth has called "pseudo-scientific portraits of social types": "the Englishman in Paris," "the drinker," "the creditor and the retailer," "the salesgirl," "the deputy," "the stevedore," and so on.[12] As books, the *physiologies* were brief, averaging around 120 pages, with thirty to sixty illustrations. While the *physiologies* were not typically comic, their format obviously derived from the same ethos that had spawned the caricature, a form that, in fact, dominated the books' visual style.

Whatever usefulness the *physiologies* purported to have rested on a single, profound faith in the reliability of appearances. As Benjamin observed of these books, "They assured people that everyone was, unencumbered by any factual knowledge, able to make out the profession, the character, the background, and the life-style of passers-by."[13] Dana Brand points out that the

plot of Poe's "The Man of the Crowd" turns on the narrator's frustrated desire to "read" the people who pass his coffeehouse window. Having identified
(at least to his own satisfaction) noblemen, merchants, attorneys, tradesmen,
stock-jobbers, clerks, pickpockets, gamblers, "Jew pedlars," professional street
beggars, invalids, prostitutes, and "ragged artisans and exhausted laborers of
every description," the narrator becomes fascinated by the illegible man to
whom none of the ready-made categories apply. Sieburth summarizes the
physiologies' appeal:

> They served to reduce the crowd's massive alterity to proportions more famil-
> iar, to transform its radical anonymity into a lexicon of nameable stereotypes,
> thereby providing their readers with the comforting illusion that the faceless
> conglomerations of the modern city could after all be read—and hence mastered
> —as a legible system of differences. ("Same Difference," 175)

This "legible system," as *S/Z* shows, is complicit with a culture's worldview: in
Barthes's words, "If we collect all such knowledge, all such vulgarisms, we create a monster, and this monster is ideology" (97). But a *New York Times* article
linking the persistence of stereotypes to their "usefulness" concludes that "the
new explorations of the cognitive role of stereotypes find them to be a distor-
tion of a process that helps people order their perceptions. The mind looks for
ways to simplify the chaos around it. Lumping people into categories is one."[14]

3.

We didn't trust ourselves at first to look long at the first
pictures [Daguerre] developed. We were abashed by the
distinctness of these human images, and believed that the
little tiny faces in the picture could see us, so powerfully
was everyone affected by the unaccustomed clarity and the
unaccustomed truth to nature of the first daguerreotypes.
—Max Dauthendey, quoted in Walter Benjamin, "A Small
History of Photography"

If the *physiologies* offered to make urban life more comfortable by first making it more legible, photography must initially have seemed part of the same
project. Soon after its discovery, the new technology became part of the pro-
liferating systems of registration and surveillance described in Benjamin's
Charles Baudelaire: A Lyric Poet in the Age of High Capitalism. Fingerprinting,
physiological measurements, and photographs recorded identity, enabled its
tracking, and circumscribed its possible escape routes into anonymity. After
photography, the kind of situation described in *The Return of Martin Guerre*,

in which a man posing as a long-vanished husband fools an entire town, appeared decisively premodern.

Like the *physiologies,* photography could boast a pseudoscientific basis and play into the late-eighteenth- and early-nineteenth-century rage for classification. But while the new technology seemed the ideal means of gathering the empirical data required by any system, almost immediately the first photographers noticed something going wrong. One historian cites Fox Talbot's surprise at what he found:

> And that was just the trouble: fascinating irrelevancy. "Sometimes inscriptions and dates are found upon buildings, or printed placards most irrelevant, are discovered upon their ways: sometimes a distant sundial is seen, and upon it— unconsciously recorded—the hour of the day at which the view was taken." To judge from his commentaries, Fox Talbot enjoyed such incidentals. At the same time, though, they were troublesome, for they meant that the instrument was only partially under control, recording disinterestedly in despite of its operator's intentions.[15]

The *physiologies* had subsumed all idiosyncrasies under the rule of the controlling term: "the banker," "the Spaniard." Indeed, their format seemed derived from La Fontaine's dictum "Nothing more common than the name, nothing rarer than the thing."[16] Photographs, on the other hand, swarming with accidental details unnoticed at the time of shooting, continually evoked precisely what eluded classification—the distinguishing feature, the contingent detail. In doing so, they undercut the *physiologies'* basic project, which photography now revealed to be committed exclusively to language as a way of understanding and ordering the world. What resisted the narrator's efforts to read the man of the crowd? "The absolute idiosyncrasy of [his] expression."[17]

By showing that every Spaniard was not dark, every banker not dull, photographs effectively criticized all classification systems and ensured that any such system attempted in photography (e.g., August Sander's) would inevitably appear not as science but as art. In fact, while the longing for strictly objective, and therefore *exact,* representation had motivated photography's invention, photographs produced precisely the opposite effect—a mute ambiguity that invited subjective reverie. Quoting the semiotician Mukarovsky, Paul Willemen has proposed that "the signifying practices having recourse to images can thus be described . . . as 'designed to render things imprecise,' as a movement towards indeterminacy."[18] Thus, photography becomes yet another example of what Edward Tenner has called the "revenge effect" of all technology: a process designed for one purpose turns out not only to subvert that purpose but to achieve its opposite.[19]

4.

Beyond the obvious facts that he has at some time done
manual labour, that he takes snuff, that he is a Freemason,
that he has been in China, and that he has done a considerable amount of writing lately, I can deduce nothing else.
　　—Sherlock Holmes in "The Red-Headed League"

That the first detective story (Poe's "The Murders in the Rue Morgue") appeared in 1841, at the height of the *physiologies* craze, and that its author felt
obliged to set his tale in Paris, a place he had never been, both suggest the
existence of an underlying connection between the two forms. In fact, the detective story represents a transposition of the physiologies, an extrapolation
from that earlier mode's purely descriptive purposes to narrative. Like the
physiologies, the detective story offered to make the world, and particularly the
urban scene, more legible. To do so, it relied incessantly on the very reference
codes the *physiologies* had propagated. Thus, for Sherlock Holmes, physical evidence is always unproblematically indexical: "the writer" will inevitably display a shiny cuff and a worn elbow patch, "the laborer" a muscular hand, "the
visitor to China" a particular Oriental tattoo.

　　Although the detective story arose almost simultaneously with the *physiologies,* it flowered only after their demise. In effect, it was not needed until later, when it functioned as an antidote to photography. "Between what
matters and what seems to matter," *Trent's Last Case* begins, "how should
the world we know judge wisely?"[20] By dramatically increasing the available
amount of particularized information, photography not only undercut the
physiologies' vulnerable, simplistic schema; it ensured that in every context
where it intervened, distinguishing the significant from the insignificant would
become treacherous. "The principal difficulty of your case," Holmes tells his
client in "The Naval Treaty," "lay in the fact of there being too much evidence"[21]—precisely the problem, the proliferation of meaning, for which Susan
Sontag blames photography:

Because each photograph is only a fragment, its moral and emotional weight
depends on where it is inserted. A photograph changes according to the context
in which it is seen. . . . And it is in this way that the presence and proliferation
of all photographs contributes to the erosion of the very notion of meaning.[22]

Thus, the first Sherlock Holmes story, "A Scandal in Bohemia," inevitably re-
vises Poe: the new threat, which the detective must find and destroy, is no
longer a purloined letter but an incriminating *photograph.*

　　And yet this story has another side, suggested, perhaps, by a coincidence
of names and a convergence of ideas:

HOLMES 1: The "distinctness of the lesser details of a building or a landscape often gives us the incidental truths which interest us more than the central object of the picture."

HOLMES 2: "If I take it up I must consider every detail. . . . Take time to consider. The smallest point may be the most essential."

Citing the first Holmes (Oliver Wendell), James Lastra proposes that photography replaced the "Albertian" hierarchy of well-made *pictures* with an "all-over" *image*, where marginal elements appear as detailed as the nominal subject. The second Holmes (Sherlock, speaking in "The Red Circle") suggests the detective story's ultimate *proximity* to photography. For, in fact, Doyle's hero depends upon a photographic way of seeing that, like rack focus, redirects the gaze from foreground to background, and, like a pan, from center to margin. In "Silver Blaze," the thrill of hearing Holmes insist on "the immense significance of the curried mutton" and "the curious incident of the dog in the nighttime" derives from having had one's attention shifted from the obvious (the gambler Fitzroy Simpson, the gypsies) to the marginal, which turns out, of course, not to be marginal at all. The Holmes stories, in other words, are the written equivalent of photographs, where apparently incidental details, like Barthes's third meanings, persistently replace the proffered *studium*. In the words of a mid-nineteenth-century writer, quoted by Lastra, "The most minute detail, which in an ordinary drawing, would merit no special attention, becomes on a photograph, worthy of careful study." Substitute "ordinary novel" for "ordinary drawing" and "in a detective story" for "on a photograph," and the connection becomes clear. Then a discovery: two days after writing these words, while visiting London's Sherlock Holmes Museum, I discover *The Unknown Conan Doyle: Essays on Photography*, a book that reveals Holmes's creator as one of late-nineteenth-century England's most avid amateur photographers.[23]

To a certain extent, the detective story differed from its predecessor, replacing the *physiologies'* intolerance for the particular with an insistence on its value. "Singularity," Holmes instructs Watson, "is almost invariably a clue. The more featureless and commonplace a crime is, the more difficult it is to bring home." What neither the detective story nor the *physiologies* can admit, however, is chance, accident, randomness—precisely those properties of all signifying systems, which, as Barthes's essay "Third Meaning" shows, photography radically enhances.[24] Every photograph, even the starkly "impoverished"[25] ones favored by advertising and propaganda, can occasion a reading that fixates on contingent details whose precise meaning eludes, at least temporarily, all readily available symbolic systems. The survival of the *physiologies* and the detective story, on the other hand, depends on the *resistance* to the accidental's appeal: if the blonde Spaniard has no place in the *physiologies*, the random crime proves fatal to the detective story—and, as Borges's "Death and the Compass" demonstrates, to the detective who wrongly insists on interpreting it. By repudiating the hermeneutic impulse in favor of the accidental, Borges's story marks the triumph of the photographic sensibility and, by implication, its most characteristic incarnation: the candid snapshot. Momentarily overcome, the anxiety to interpret, which had prompted both the *physiologies* and the detective story, returns in *Blow-Up*, where it is ironically evoked by exactly such snapshots that now reveal a crime. But while the movie cites the detective-story form, it refuses to subordinate images to language, suggesting with its inconclusive ending that the need to explain must ultimately be abandoned.

5.

In the history of films, every great moment that shines is a silent one.
—King Vidor, quoted in Joseph Cotten, *Vanity Will Get You Somewhere: An Autobiography*

Without its [inner speech's] function of binding subject and text in sociality [some system of shared meanings produced by shared codes], no signification would be possible other than delirium.
—Paul Willemen, "Cinematic Discourse"

At the origins of photography, therefore, lies an intersection of related problems: the legibility of the surrounding world, the status of the detail, the relationship between image and language. For the *physiologies* and the detective story, rituals of the word's mastery over things, photography represents the other that must be contained. In the twentieth century, this contest finds a new site—the cinema.

Filmmaking has, from the first, been shaped by the answers proposed to a set of fundamental questions: How do we make sense of a film? What happens when we encounter a movie segment for the first time? How do we process cinematic information? During the experimental phase of Soviet cinema, Boris Eikhenbaum suggested, in an especially influential answer, that we accompany our film watching with an "inner speech." In particular, inner speech makes the connection between separate shots. A useful example occurs in *Born Free*'s opening scene, which cuts back and forth between a woman washing clothes in a river and a stalking lion, apparently intent on an unseen prey. With the woman and the lion never appearing together in any frame, the sequence culminates in three shots: the lion springs, the woman turns and screams, and the river rushes away, now littered with clothes and a spreading red stain. The scene's meaning is clear: the lion has killed the woman. That meaning, however, while an *effect* of the images, appears nowhere in them. It occurs only in the viewer's mind, whose inner speech responds to the movie's images and sounds with the linguistic formulation "lion kills woman."

The notion of inner speech reaffirms, in Paul Willemen's words, "the interdependence of the verbal and the visual in cinema."[26] Even the nonverbal is grasped in relation to the verbal, which translates it into our dominant meaning system, language. Significantly, the concept of inner speech arises with silent film and in a genre (propaganda) in which unambiguous communication is the goal. In that context, what is most feared is the capacity of images to produce not meaning but what Willemen calls "delirium." Without a verbal soundtrack to anchor the images and constrain their potential drift, and with the continuity rules still inchoate, inner speech had to rely on other visual elements for the verbal formulations that would bind the unrolling pictures into a coherent statement.

Recognizing their images' potential for ambiguity and imprecision, silent-era filmmakers structured their shots around formulaic characters, sequences, and even verbal expressions. The silent cinema, in fact, represents the single most important revival of the *physiologies.* There we again encounter the *physiologies'* basic assumption that every character type has its own unvarying physical embodiment: villains look villainous (with moustaches and squinting eyes), heroines look virtuous (with petticoats and blonde hair), and businessmen look businesslike (with suits and starched shirtfronts). Very early in the movies' evolution, filmmaking also gravitated to stock actions—the chase, the lovers' meeting, the deathbed vigil. In *S/Z*, Barthes designates such predictable sequences as part of the "proairetic code," that reservoir of generic actions such as "the stroll," "the murder," or "the rendezvous" (Barthes's examples) that trigger ready-made inner speech; indeed, Barthes proposes that this "code of actions principally determines the readability of the text" (*S/Z*, 262). At its most extreme subservience to language, a silent film's image track would occasionally provide a *visual* translation of a stock phrase: *October*'s juxtaposition of the provisional dictator Kerensky with a mechanical peacock ("proud as a peacock") is only the most famous example of this device.

Sound moviemaking did not abandon these formulae; it simply relied on newly developed strategies for making them subtler. Most useful were Hollywood's continuity protocols, founded on the two principles of matching and centering, both designed to overcome film's fundamental discontinuity. While the matching rules ensured that editing would connect shots by means of certain cinematic grammar, centering guaranteed that all *mise-en-scène* elements (e.g., lighting, framing, shot size) would visually underline narratively impor-

3–12. Sequence from *Born Free*

tant events. To the extent that the continuity rules circumscribed the movies' images, regulated their meaning in terms of a single narrative, and vastly reduced their potential complexity, they became, like the detective story, *a means of policing photography*—and another example of language's control of the image.

While the notion of inner speech arises in film's infancy, Barthes's "third meaning" appears in its maturity. With its insistence on perverse readings that ignore, and indeed refuse, intended or contextually obvious significances, the third-meaning disposition clearly descends from Surrealist tactics designed to reassert the autonomy and ambiguity of images: think again, for example, of Man Ray's habit of watching the screen through his fingers, spread to isolate certain parts of the image; of Breton's advocacy of eating and talking during showings as means for reorienting one's attention to the marginal incident or detail; of Breton's weekend moviegoing:

When I was "at the cinema age" (it should be recognized that this age exists in life—and that it passes) I never began by consulting the amusement pages to find out what film might chance to be the best, nor did I find out the time the film was to begin. I agreed wholeheartedly with Jacques Vaché in appreciating nothing so much as dropping into the cinema when whatever was playing was playing, at any point in the show, and leaving at the first hint of boredom—of surfeit—to rush off to another cinema where we behaved in the same way. . . . I have never known anything more *magnetizing;* it goes without saying that more often than not we left our seats without even knowing the title of the film, which was of no importance to us anyway. On a Sunday several hours sufficed to exhaust all that Nantes could offer us: the important thing is that one came out "charged" for a few days.[27]

Both Barthes's "third meaning" practice and the Surrealist strategies of film-watching amount to methods of *extraction, fragmentation.* In both, the individual segment, image, or detail is isolated from the narrative that would circumscribe it. "To a certain extent," Barthes proposes, the third meaning "cannot be grasped in the projected film, the film 'in movement,' '*au naturel,*' but only, as yet, in that major artifact which is the still."[28] Like the detective story, Hollywood filmmaking (still the international norm) "arrests the multiplication of meanings," as D. A Miller argues, "by uniquely privileging one of them"[29]—that set designated "significant" by the unrolling story. In his autobiography, Barthes acknowledged his own "resistance to the cinema," attributing it to the "statutory impossibility of the fragment" in a continuous, "saturated" medium.[30]

Narrative, in fact, subordinates its images to the linguistic formulations they serve. "The sequence exists," Barthes writes of the action code, "when

13. Still from *Andy Hardy Gets Spring Fever*

and because it can be given a name" (*S/Z*, 19). Thus, encountering a picture offering itself as "a still," we will immediately begin to imagine the missing story. Doing so typically involves a summoning of the received categories stored in inner speech, the "already-done," the "already-read." If, for example, we were to come across the accompanying still from *Andy Hardy Gets Spring Fever*, to what plot would we imagine it belonging? a sad love story? a tale of vampires? a mystery? To the extent that any of these constructions would immediately limit the image's possibilities, we can make this proposition: in late-twentieth-century civilization, every image lies surrounded by invisible formulae whose inevitable activation reasserts our stubborn allegiance to language as the only means of making sense.

Artists have begun to play with this situation, implying the traps into which our preference for language leads us. Cindy Sherman's "Film Stills" have become the most famous case, a complex use of photography, disguise, and the word "still" to imply movies that do not in fact exist—and to snare the viewer into "explaining" the photographs in terms of the cinematic conventions (e.g., *film noir*, Antonioniesque angst, Southern Gothic) already available to inner speech. Equally suggestive is Chris Van Allsburg's children's book *The Mysteries of Harris Burdick*, a collection of fourteen captioned images, each purporting to be the single remaining illustration of stories never found.

What is at stake with this relationship between language and image? The research tradition that Derrida calls "grammatology" posits that different technologies of communication occasion different ways of thinking. An oral culture, for example, relying entirely on human memory to store and retrieve its information, develops conceptual habits that would appear strange to us, the inhabitants of a fully alphabetic society. Grammatology further suggests that human history has seen only two major revolutions in communications technology: the first involved precisely this shift from oral to alphabetic cultures; the second, the transition from alphabetic to "electronic" or "cinematic," we are living through now. What are the consequences, characteristics, and modes of an age of photography, film, television, magnetic tape, and computers? How will what we call thinking change with this technology?

It will be up to us to decide. And here the matter of language and photography intervenes decisively. To the extent that such deciding will require invention, the persistence of formulae becomes inhibiting. The "already-read" categories of the *physiologies,* the detective story, and inner speech seek to define the new technology (photography, film) in terms of the old (language), thereby restricting our capacity to admit the full implications of the revolution surrounding us. Roger Cardinal calls this way of dealing with images the "literate mode," derived from "habits of purposeful reading of texts" and assuming that "the artist has centred or signalled his image in accordance with the conventions of representation" so that "the viewer's gaze will be attuned to that focal message and will ignore its periphery." The alternative, one that "focuses less narrowly and instead roams over the frame, sensitive to its textures and surfaces," Cardinal associates with "non-literacy and with habits of looking which are akin to habits of touching."[31] This way of putting the matter seems absolutely consistent with the tradition we might call, following Sontag, "against interpretation." Surrealism, Barthes's "third meaning" essay, and photography itself have all explicitly evoked eroticism as an analogue for a new practice of the image. If that practice involves, as *Blow-Up* suggests, a relaxation of the explanatory drive (our version of the will-to-power?), its motto might result from changing one word in the dictum thrown like a knife at the literary establishment almost thirty years ago, ironically by one who has become photography's enemy: in place of a hermeneutics we need an erotics, not of art, but of photography.[32]

A most remarkable change in our ideas is taking place, one
of such rapidity that it seems to promise a greater change
still to come. It will be for the future to decide the aim, the
nature and the limits of this revolution, and the drawbacks
and disadvantages of which posterity will be able to judge
better than we can.

—D'Alembert (1759)[1]

3 The Bordwell Regime and the Stakes of Knowledge

I. What Counts as Romance?

In the spring of 1984 at the University of Florida, I saw a poster that, in
hindsight, seems an emblem of the late-twentieth-century cultural condition
we call postmodernism. Advertising a local band capriciously (predictably?)
named the Vulgar Boatmen, the poster consisted mainly of a single large image: a street scene in marked chiaroscuro, where an elegantly dressed, solitary
woman, photographed from behind and at a considerable distance, moved in
silhouette across cobblestones toward a tram emerging from a zone whose
specifics had escaped the camera, framed in a Gothic arch delineating an in-
exact brightness. Underneath was the caption *What counts as Romance?* The
pun in the band's name, the appropriated image (whose previous contexts, the

14. Josef Sudek

highbrow culture of its unnamed Steiglitz-styled photographer [the Czech Josef Sudek] and the cover of a book on East European dissent, imply the now typical migration from art to politics to pop), even the picture's potential (and corny) allegory of an unknown, simultaneously promising and menacing future—all these things have become commonplace. I am more immediately interested, however, in the caption, for as with any such major shift, the transition from modernism to postmodernism entails an anxiety about *what counts.*

Around this anxiety turn two of postmodernism's central texts, Borges's "Pierre Menard, Author of the Quixote" and Kuhn's *Structure of Scientific Revolutions.* While Borges uses postmodernism's great aesthetic object, the readymade, to ask, *What counts as art?* Kuhn invokes history's shifting definitions of science to demonstrate how differently we have answered the apparently simple question *What counts as knowledge?* Indeed, although purporting simply to describe science's impermanent epistemology, Kuhn in fact epitomized what Lyotard later diagnosed as the basic postmodern situation, "the crisis of legitimation."[2]

In many ways, modernism began with Auguste Comte's attempts to specify what counts as knowledge. His definition, elaborated in the philosophy he called positivist, was ironically a formalism, since for Comte, "truth" depended less on a proposition's matching the observed world than on its having resulted from a particular investigatory procedure. A refined version of Baconian empirical science, Comte's method started with the elimination of "theological" or "metaphysical" questions, deemed unanswerable (and therefore impeding) because they sought ultimate explanations for phenomena. This reduction of inquiry's scope Comte regarded as the "main characteristic" of positivism, whose optimism about clearing up what was left makes its founder seem like Judge Hardy:

In the positive state, the human mind, recognizing the impossibility of obtaining absolute truth, gives up the search after the origin and hidden causes of the universe and a knowledge of the final causes of phenomena. It endeavours now only to discover, by a well-combined use of reasoning and observation, the actual laws of phenomena—that is to say, their invariable relations of succession and likeness. The explanation of facts, thus reduced to its real terms, consists henceforth only in the connection established between different particular phenomena and some general facts, the number of which the progress of science tends more and more to diminish.[3]

Although Comte couched this curtailment of questioning as a modest appeal to reason ("No sensible person would nowadays seek to go beyond this" [9]), positivism's self-confidence ultimately committed it to an intellectual terrorism against its chief opponents:

[T]he whole social mechanism rests finally on opinions. . . . [T]he great political and moral crisis of existing societies is due at bottom to intellectual anarchy. Our gravest evil consists, indeed, in this profound divergence that now exists among all minds. . . . As long as individual minds are not unanimously agreed upon a certain number of general ideas capable of forming a common social doctrine, we cannot disguise the fact that the nations will necessarily remain in an essentially revolutionary state. . . .

[T]he actual confusion of men's minds is at bottom due to the simultaneous employment of three radically incompatible philosophies—the theological, the metaphysical, and the positive. It is quite clear that, if any one of these three philosophies really obtained a complete and universal preponderance, a fixed social order would result. . . . Now, if this opinion be correct, all that is necessary is to know which of the three philosophies can and must prevail by the nature of things; every sensible man should next endeavor to work for the triumph of that philosophy. . . . (28–29)

Since Comte regarded the positive philosophy "as constituting the only solid basis of . . . social reorganization" (28), he naturally pressed for its adoption as the universal standard. In doing so, Comte was implicitly reviving Voltaire, especially the Voltaire whose "Remarks on M. Pascal's Thoughts" had insisted on separating solvable, practical questions from impenetrable, metaphysical ones. This strategy's reappearance in Wittgenstein's famous conclusion to the *Tractatus* ("What we cannot speak about we must pass over in silence"[4]) confirms modernism's connection to neoclassicism, a link most visible in their architectural styles.

For both modernism and classicism, the enemy is the *baroque*, understood in its broadest sense to include mannerism and the rococo. Indeed, Heinrich Wölfflin proposed the classic-baroque opposition as art history's permanent structure, with one mode replacing the other in a cyclical alternation of dominance.[5] From this perspective, cultural movements line up in one of the two camps:

Classic	*Baroque*
Renaissance	Mannerism/Baroque/Rococo
Neo-Classicism	Romanticism
Positivism/Realism/Naturalism	Symbolism/Decadence
Modernism	Postmodernism

Defining itself oppositionally, the baroque has typically recognized classicism's necessity as the older, responsible, predictable brother in a family never disowned. Classicism, on the other hand, has never accepted the baroque as a legitimate alternative, associating it from the start (in Diderot's *Encyclopedia* entry) with the superficial, the "bizarre," the "abusive," the "ridiculous pushed to excess."[6] For classicism, the baroque remains the style, as Wölfflin put it, "into which the Renaissance degenerated."[7]

Etymologically, however, the baroque is valuable, deriving not only from a logical term connoting absurdity,[8] but also from a French word meaning "irregular pearl."[9] In fact, contemporary culture typically prefers the baroque terms in Wölfflin's famous conceptual pairs:[10]

Classic	*Baroque*
linear	painterly
plane	recession
closed	open
clearless	clear

That preference should not surprise us, for postmodernism and poststructuralism represent precisely a revival of the baroque, as translating Wölfflin's terms from painting to writing confirms. An emphasis on style, a propensity for digression, an aptitude for inconclusiveness, a toleration of obliqueness—these dispositions characterize poststructuralism's leading texts, from *Écrits* to *A Lover's Discourse* to *Glas*. Dismissing the baroque's productions as irregular, capricious, illogical, and structureless,[11] classicism affirms the hierarchical opposition described by Barthes: "on the one side the 'thought', object of the message, element of knowledge, transitive or critical force; on the other the 'style', ornament, province of luxury and leisure and thus futility."[12] Classicism: the signified:: the baroque: the signifier?

However tempting that formulation may be, the matter is historically less simple. For while classicism has always appropriated a certain version of science to enhance its own prestige (see, for example, Zola's *Experimental Novel*), natural science itself and the philosophy derived from it were, as Arnold Hauser reminds us, inventions of the baroque. Even mannnerism, baroque's infancy, previously discredited as trivially devoted to style, now seems founded on questions basic to science. "Mannerism," Hauser suggests in *The Social History of Art*, "is the first modern style, the first which is concerned with a cultural problem and which regards the relationship between tradition and innovation as a problem to be solved by rational means" (100).

Both classicism and the baroque produce knowledge. The questions are *how?* and *what kind?* In effect, classicism represents normal science, the implementation of ideas whose revolutionary formulations typically involve baroque strategies: new metaphors ("survival of the fittest"), refocused attention (from the cause of biological varieties to their selection), interdisciplinary borrowing (see the recent merger of biology and electronics).[13] The baroque revives when the effectiveness of a particular classicism begins to wane. What gets abandoned is not knowledge *tout court,* but classicism's insistence on a single investigative method. The most explicit statement of the baroque's relationship to knowledge appears in Breton's 1924 *Surrealist Manifesto:*

We are still living under the reign of logic, but the logical processes of our time apply only to the solutions of problems of secondary interest. The absolute rationalism which remains in fashion allows for the consideration of only those facts narrowly relevant to our experience. . . . Needless to say, boundaries have been assigned even to experience. . . . and we have proscribed every way of seeking the truth which does not conform to convention. . . . Perhaps the imagination is on the verge of recovering its rights. If the depths of our minds conceal strange forces capable of augmenting or conquering those on the surface, it is in our greatest interest to capture them; first to capture them and later to submit them, should the occasion arise, to the control of reason. . . . But it is important to note that there is no method fixed *a priori* for the execution of this enterprise, that until the new order it can be considered the province of poets as well as scholars, and that its success does not depend upon the more or less capricious routes which will be followed.[14]

"We are not your enemies," Apollinaire insisted, writing as the man who had invented the word "surrealism" about what he called "this long quarrel of tradition and innovation / Of Order and Adventure."[15] But the very strangeness of ideas derived by unconventional means inevitably provokes classicists who recognize only certain kinds of knowledge. Think, for example, of how undergraduates, typically steeped in the prevailing classicism's definition of legitimacy, regard incredulously Freud's "Signorelli" analysis.[16] For them, an explanation of forgetting derived less from physiology (or common sense) than poetics, one attending to certain words' audible similarities, seems thoroughly unscientific. Nearly a century after Freud's incident, extrapolations from his work (e.g., Derrida's "puncepts,"[17] Barthes's interrogation of the letters S and Z) still do not count as knowledge for most people.

Why not? If we are indeed in the midst of a widely announced paradigm shift into postmodernism, what accounts for the abiding resistance to non-Baconian knowledge? If "invention is always born of dissension,"[18] if knowledge depends on a willingness to investigate the implications of strategies that initially seem bizarre, why have many academic fields so abandoned experimentation that, as Lyotard maintains in *The Postmodern Condition*, "it is safe to say that responsibility for it will devolve upon extrauniversity networks" (50)?

Any answer to these questions would necessarily address the extent to which late-twentieth-century knowledge has become an effect of institutions. Moving from general to specific, I would make the following points: (1) While information has always been a commodity, regulated by the institutions it traverses, the last 150 years of mass-media growth have accelerated the speed of assimilation and co-option beyond the Enlightenment's wildest dreams. We do not yet fully understand this event's impact on knowledge. We do know that the mass media simultaneously crave and trivialize novelty, whose rapid circulation in reduced form both serves and inhibits knowledge. Indeed, television as a frame is the ultimate *passe-partout*,[19] allowing the baroque to circulate within a context that seeks to defuse it: think of the network show *Ripley's Believe It or Not*, hosted by Marie Osmond (!), which gave prime time to avant-garde performance artists, albeit presented as bizarre spectacles. (2) Academic institutions, thoroughly subject to mass media's influence (via computers, television, publishing), have their own inertia, resulting from systems of tenure, promotion, and granting that largely encourage what Lyotard calls "diminished tasks of research" conducted under prevailing conventions.[20] (3) Twenty years of Ph.D. oversupply has magnified the power of accepted procedures and made academics even more cautious. Can one imagine an untenured Freud submitting *The Psychopathology of Everyday Life* as research?

In what follows I will examine one particular institution, Anglo-American film studies, and the effect of one of its leading figures, David Bordwell of the University of Wisconsin. I should say at the outset that although I may at times seem critical of Bordwell and his work, I have the highest admiration for both. In fact, his case is worth studying precisely because he is the best at what he does.

Bordwell is a classicist, in some ways film studies' Voltaire: prolific, brilliant, and combative. Not surprisingly, he uses the words "Baroque," "Mannerist," and "rococo" as pejoratives and generally denounces "the arid heights of Theory."[21] The Deconstructionists, he argues in "Adventures in the Highlands of Theory," "threaten to turn theory utterly relativist and dilettantish" (97). Like all classicists, Bordwell admires the Baconian empirical model of hypotheses-tested-against-evidence, and he has scrupulously applied its exacting standards to himself. "There comes a point," he has insisted, "where a theoretical formulation must not simply cite presuppositions and select privileged instances but test itself against a body of detailed evidence."[22] Indeed, his description of his own *modus operandi* exactly matches Kuhn's picture of normal science: "for me, at least, research begins with puzzles that I think worth solving"; and "one should strive for *an argument to the best explanation*."[23]

This commitment to a classical research program has resulted in an extraordinarily impressive body of work, culminating in an early *magnum opus, The Classical Hollywood Cinema: Film Style and Mode of Production to 1960* (*CHC*), co-authored with Janet Staiger and Kristin Thompson.[24] This book's explanation of how the pre-1908 "primitive cinema" of Edwin S. Porter et al. evolved (or mutated) into "the movies," Hollywood's narrative mode that conquered the world, rests on the most mammoth empirical research effort film studies has seen: Bordwell, Staiger, and Thompson (BST) have watched more films and read more about their making than anyone else. They pointedly rely on a computer-generated random sample of films, a gesture of scientificity that, as Michel de Certeau has pointed out, compels belief "by citing a source of power": using a computer becomes the twentieth-century equivalent of the Renaissance "Dedication to the Prince," "a recognition of obligations with respect to the power that overdetermines the rationality of an epoch."[25]

CHC's massive evidentiary base and his own arguments with other film historians betray Bordwell's symptomatic obsession with legitimation. What counts for him are propositions confirmed by facts. You may disagree with our conclusions, he repeatedly argues, but for your disagreement to count, you must come up with proof. No one has been able to do so because on his own ground, Bordwell seems irrefutable. Indeed, this kind of response is foredoomed, because Bordwell has anticipated it. Since *CHC*'s exposition often depends on tactically discrediting previous film historians (e.g., André Bazin, Jean-Louis Comolli)—an orientation "toward the negative" that de Certeau identified as history's basic trope[26]—we must acknowledge BST's willingness to live by the sword, and assume that they have marshaled the protective evidence needed to keep from dying by it. In 1983, Bordwell and Thompson cleared the way for *CHC* by attacking the accuracy of the theoretical project most resembling their own: Noël Burch's account of how Hollywood managed to make its version the cinematic norm.[27] Burch, Bordwell and Thompson argued, got his dates wrong, ignored primary sources, and generalized from atypical movies. Having liquidated Burch with facts, Bordwell and Thompson were not likely to have allowed *CHC* to appear prematurely. Barthes once observed that scholarly writing aspiring to science's objectivity and rigor inevitably advances under the signs of *precaution*,[28] and again and again BST cover their tracks: multiplying examples and citing sources, especially the trade publications of Hollywood's lighting, sound, and camera technicians.

Given that *CHC* is well written, thoroughly researched, eminently reasonable, and that BST are among the brightest people working in film studies, picking away at the book's minor points or omissions seems pointless. Indeed, Bordwell's devastating reply to *CHC*'s reviewers confirms that approach's futility. In any case, knowledge, as Lyotard notes, does not often issue from mere adversariness:

[E]veryone knows that a countermove that is merely reactional is not a "good" move. Reactional countermoves are no more than programmed effects in the opponent's strategy; they play into his hands and thus have no effect on the balance of power. That is why it is important to increase displacement in the game, and even to disorient it, in such a way as to make an unexpected move" (a new statement).[29]

In refusing to make "an unexpected move," *CHC*'s reviewers, while often intending a critique of Bordwell's alleged ideological inattentiveness, in fact merely enhanced his reputation. For Bordwell's typical reply not only trumps the book's critics; it also manages to advertise BST's most important books and articles.[30]

What would "an unexpected move" be? Let me try this one: I will not argue with David Bordwell. Instead, I am interested in what might happen if I take a different tack and *change the subject* (as a student might move from one academic department to another), using *CHC* not as an occasion to debate its conclusion (with which I agree) but to speculate about what we think of as knowledge, how it develops and circulates among disciplines, and how it is transmitted by our pedagogy and writing. I am gambling that *CHC* is precisely *not* an atypical work, but rather one that represents prevalent assumptions about knowledge and its dissemination. While the book obviously sympto- mizes the current state of film studies, it may also tell us something about clas- sicism's effect on what many people in the humanities are now calling "the crisis of knowledge."

2. Regimes of Knowledge

For the job:
1) You think about it.
2) You figure it all out.
3) You tell everybody.
4) You do it.
5) You buy the paint.
6) You check everything.
7) You paint it.
8) You recheck everything.
9) You work the whole thing over some more.
10) You make it go.
         —Nicholas, in Godard's *Married Woman*

Neither classicism nor the baroque has any inherent political disposition; con- text always proves decisive.[31] In 1715, neoclassicism was radical; in 1800, it was not. But if we have begun to sense modernism's end, we should start asking how continued allegiance to classical research models now influences knowl- edge. One thing is clear: Bordwell in general, and *CHC* in particular, are seen as having immense influence over their domain. One reviewer insisted that *CHC* "is going to change the way American film history is studied"; and an- other that the book "is quite simply the single most important publishing event in the field of American film history to occur within the last twenty-five years."[32]

Exactly what kind of event is *CHC*? In the first place, it is an argument that runs like this: Platonic/teleological histories of the cinema (associated most prominently with Bazin and Lewis Jacobs) were wrong. They assumed a realistic/narrative essence of the cinema toward which filmmaking inevitably, albeit asymptotically, advanced. While this position made sense from hind- sight (after all, most films we get to see *are* "realistic" narratives), the cinema could have been any number of other things: visual lyric, documentary, a new form of vaudeville, formalist experimentation, political intervention, etc. In the struggle for cultural dominance, however, the cinematic variation that privileged storytelling won out and became for the vast majority of the audi- ence, both here and abroad, the apparent definition of the medium itself. The name for that variation is "Classical Hollywood Cinema." Hollywood's hegemony has been so thoroughgoing that to a certain extent, the significance of many of film history's great figures might be said to have arisen simply from their willingness to pursue one or more of the cinema's excluded modes: e.g., Vigo, the lyric; Vertov, the experimental documentary; Eisenstein, the experimental political film. In truth, we cannot really measure these filmmakers' success, for while the *auteur* theory long ago maintained that one could make distinctions among the vast melting pot of storytellers, those working in the alternative modes have never faced much competition.

Far from arising out of some intrinsic essence of cinema, Hollywood's variation depended on particular strategies resulting from a unique coincidence of historical determinations. Strikingly, in both its formal and thematic procedures, the Hollywood Cinema sought to conceal that fact, developing protocols that consistently minimized the necessity for deciding between alternatives. Formally, Hollywood's "invisible style" (the continuity system of matching, centering, shot-reverse shot, the 180-degree rule, etc.), by making each shot and sequence appear inevitable, hid the dozens of choices required by *mise-en-scène* and editing. Thematically, by preferring plots that turned on oppositions ultimately resolved, its genre tradition obscured the choices demanded by material circumstances. Like most recent film historians, BST work from the premise that Hollywood's triumph, a historical event, is massively overdetermined, reflecting the histories of technology, economics, competing commercial forms, individual filmmakers and financiers, other media, politics, and the mass audience. As a discourse, film theory, in effect, amounts to a long-running debate about the emphasis to be assigned each of these determinants: if film history involves a materially influenced evolution, which of these factors is the equivalent of natural selection? While the *auteurists* argued the primacy of individual filmmaking geniuses (outside the Hollywood system, or working in quiet, subtle revolt within it, in what Manny Farber called "termite art"), and Marxists such as Burch insist on the dominance of bourgeois ideology and capitalist economics, BST as late entrants in the quarrel refuse simplistic explanations. For them, the cinema is a distinct formation of its own, albeit one subject to the uneven development of the material domains in which it is enmeshed. While less dramatic than hard-line *auteurism*, Marxism, or McLuhan's technological determinism, this conclusion seems unassailable. It also allows BST to demonstrate that Classical Hollywood Cinema's roots in so many different materialities have given it extraordinary staying power and the capacity to assimilate even the most critical deviations, appearing in what Bordwell designates as the three principal alternatives to Hollywood practice: the "art," "avant-garde," and "modernist" cinemas (381).

For all the fanfare attending *CHC*'s publication, these conclusions are remarkably predictable. The argument has been fine-tuned since Burch and Comolli began it, the dates gotten right, the non-teleological position reemphasized, the empirical base deepened, but I cannot imagine that many film scholars reasonably familiar with the discipline would be surprised by *CHC*'s position. This kind of slowing down, the retreat from saltations to carefully considered increments, signals a discipline's emergence (or decline) into "normal science"; and *CHC*'s very shape, its size and weight, indicate the kind of textbook closure only possible in a field that has settled down.[33]

In fact (!), the book's reception confirms the abiding dominance of Comtean Standards. As a group, *CHC*'s reviewers seemed less impressed by the book's conclusion than by the apparatus used to generate it. With its computer samples, scores of obscure movie and periodical citations, four appendices, and sixty-five double-columned pages of footnotes, *CHC* dramatically foregrounds its own claims to objectivity. As a book, it is simultaneously modest and vain: not a personally expressive "structuration" (Barthes's own term for *S/Z*) of film history, but the impersonally accurate *truth* about the Hollywood Cinema, or at least more of that truth than we have had before. Foucault, however (following Nietzsche), encouraged us to suspect such claims, insisting that truth and knowledge are less empirical categories than political ones, "system[s] of ordered procedures for the production, regulation, distribution, circulation, and operation of statements"[34]—not *methods* of truth and knowledge, in other words, but *regimes:*

[T]ruth isn't outside power, or lacking in power: contrary to a myth whose history and functions would repay further study, truth isn't the reward of free spirits, the child of protracted solitude, nor the privilege of those who have succeeded in liberating themselves. Truth is a thing of this world: it is produced only by virtue of multiple forms of constraint. And it induces regular effects of power. Each society has its regime of truth, "its general politics" of truth: that is, the types of discourses which it accepts and makes function as true; the mechanisms and instances which enable one to distinguish true and false statements, the means by which each is sanctioned; the techniques and procedures accorded value in the acquisition of truth; the status of those charged with saying what counts as true. (*The Foucault Reader*, 72–73)

Each of these elements in what Brecht termed an "apparatus" (a socially authorized mode of producing, distributing, consuming, and evaluating information)[35] is implicated in "power," Foucault's Nietzschean word for what we more often call "politics" or "ideology": "power," however, effectively suggests the contested nature of even naturalized regimes like those of truth and knowledge. Whose voice will be warranted as conveying "knowledge"? How did he or she acquire credibility? What factors will enhance or erode that credibility? Such questions imply the competitive, exclusionary aspect of these regimes: BST win our assent at the expense of others who thereby lose it. If BST provide us with "knowledge," then their enemies (let us say, Noël Burch) must have been leading us astray.

In a professionally competitive environment like American academics, one distinguished by the instantaneous and pervasive circulation of information, opinions, and gossip, knowledge becomes even more inseparable from power. A handful of prestigious scholars are repeatedly enlisted to referee tenure and promotion decisions, edit journals, and screen submitted manuscripts. Above all, these scholars attract students, enlistees in existing research programs. As Lyotard points out, teaching plays an enormous role in perpetuating institutional norms:

> It should be evident that research appeals to teaching as its necessary complement: the scientist needs an addressee who can in turn become the sender; he needs a partner. Otherwise the verification of statements would be impossible. . . . One's competence is never an accomplished fact. It depends on whether or not the statement proposed is considered by one's peers to be worth discussion in a sequence of argumentation and refutation. The truth of the statement and the competence of its sender are thus subject to the collective approval of a group of persons who are competent on an equal basis. Equals are needed and must be created.
>
> Didactics is what ensures that this reproduction takes place.[36]

I am not offering a conspiracy theory or decrying knowledge's institutionalization; I am merely describing a situation furthered in postmodernism. In fact, the dominant figures in American film studies, especially Bordwell, conduct themselves with the strictest probity. But their power should not be minimized.

Bordwell's own case reveals how a particular regime of knowledge constitutes itself by participation in (and citation of) a culture's institutions and covenants. To be specific: from 1980 until the present, the territory of American film studies has been divided up between two *caporegimes,* those of the University of Iowa's Dudley Andrew and the University of Wisconsin's David Bordwell. These men attained their stature in the obvious ways: prolific, high-quality publication; active leadership within the discipline's main organization (the Society for Cinema Studies); skillful teaching; and regular attendance at conferences. Of these factors, the publication record clearly has the most weight, but in characterizing Bordwell's published work as "high quality," I have already begun to beg the kinds of questions Foucault poses about knowledge's relationship to power. To say that Bordwell has greater credibility than others who have published even more because his work is "good" should not satisfy us if we want to understand how knowledge circulates among us. Why do we find it "good"?

One answer is simple: Bordwell's work, like that of almost everyone designated by our culture as providing "knowledge," participates thoroughly in the apparatus that Nietzsche describes as Western civilization's last great religion: rational science.[37] As a writer, Bordwell is classically clear. He eschews "excessive" metaphors and obviously bravura figures (the signs of his own desire), thereby avoiding the fate of Michelet, whose devotion to the signifier prompted his demotion from history to literature.[38] Bordwell's preference for active verbs and clearly defined transitions reaffirms the rational tradition's faith in cause-and-effect sequences of distinct, locatable events. Even the format of his books, maintained through several volumes, is scientific: double-columned, oversized, they literally stand out from the rest of a shelf of ordinary humanities books, manifesting the signs of textbook authority amidst the clutter of mere "interpretations." Indeed, Bordwell's prose and format mime *CHC*'s subject: he and his coauthors produced the book equivalent of the widescreen, "invisible style," cause-and-effect–linked Hollywood movie.

Like all information certified by a culture as "knowledge," Bordwell's work coincided with the interests of a particular community at a particular moment. Such *matching* is always necessary according to Thomas Kuhn, who points to Aristarchus's anticipation of Copernican heliocentrism, unheeded for eighteen centuries because it corresponded to no group's urgent needs.[39] Sometime about 1975, two years after the English translation of Noël Burch's *Theory of Film Practice*, the formalist Bible (Burch is an American but usually writes in French), the American film studies community finally decided that it wanted to know about cinematic grammar: the spatial/temporal articulations possible in editing, the strategies of framing, the juxtapositions of sound and image, etc. (If 1975 seems rather late to arrive at such fundamental questions, we should remember that as a discipline, film studies is both recent and mongrel, many of its members having begun as literary scholars.) Bordwell's own intellectual maturity occurred as his field developed interests that were his own. If one wants to know, for example, about the spatial discontinuities that make Dreyer's *Vampyr* so difficult, Bordwell's discussion is extraordinarily useful.[40] Similarly, his eighty-two-page description of Classical Hollywood's formal protocols should satisfy anyone needing a clear but subtle primer of American movie grammar.[41]

To a certain extent, Bordwell's work might have found an audience in previous eras of film studies. As a thorough student with a supple mind, he has inevitably absorbed the basic elements of previous American approaches. Thus, while Bordwell has consistently used formalism as an organizing emphasis, each of his books could fit into at least one other category. *Filmguide to "La Passion de Jeanne d'Arc"* (1973), *The Films of Carl-Theodor Dreyer* (1981), *Ozu and the Poetics of Cinema* (1988), and *The Cinema of Eisenstein* (1993) obviously attend to individual films and filmmakers, but they also contribute to a film history that singles out particular accomplishments and to the discipline's oxymoronic "*auteur*-structuralism," which encourages critics to detect recurring motifs in a director's work. As textbooks, Bordwell and Thompson's *Film Art* (1979) and *Film History: An Introduction* (1994) necessarily review the cinema's history, as *Making Meaning* (1989) does that of film studies itself. *CHC*, explicitly a history of Hollywood's form, grounds itself in a much-refined version of *Jump Cut*'s often vulgar materialism. Finally, *Narration in the Fiction Film* (1985) and *On the History of Film Style* (1997) subject even Bordwell's privileged formalism to a history-of-ideas approach while simultaneously using it to read individual movies.

This apparent eclecticism, however, is offset by a characteristic of normal science: a disciplinary specialization that marks itself in *repetition*. Whatever approach he takes, Bordwell pursues film study; moreover, to the extent that he succeeds in establishing a single, persistently used method, he becomes reliable, *predictable* (positivism's goal): a brand name to depend on.[42] Constituted by repetition, scientific regimes of knowledge censor the unanticipated and discourage vocational wandering: the specialist leaving his area of expertise not only loses his rights to convey "knowledge"; he also discredits his own previous work (see the case of Linus Pauling). As what Foucault calls a "specific intellectual," an expert or savant,[43] Bordwell can thus speak on "universal" issues only to the extent that they intersect with *film studies*. Were he to move only slightly away from his established domain—to write, let us say, a book on Hemingway—he would risk undermining what he has already done.

While some intellectuals chafe at the knowledge regime's demand for repetition (see Roland Barthes, who made that demand, and his own outmaneuvering of it, his autobiographical subjects), Bordwell welcomes it. Indeed, he would have us further narrow (at least temporarily) the domain of film studies and restrict its practitioners to a single paradigm (formalism) for the sake of orderly empirical investigation and validation. Bordwell urged this consolidation in a short article that functions as the *sub silentio* program underlying *CHC*: "Lowering the Stakes: Prospects for a Historical Poetics of Cinema."[44] A curious word, *stake:* in one definition, a theological *regime* (a Mormon territory ruled by a single bishop); in another, *an instrument of death,* for Dreyer's Jeanne d'Arc (burned at one) and the vampire (killed by one driven into the heart).

3. The "Stakes" in Film Studies: Knowledge as a Terrain, a Gamble, a Share; Knowledge as Moving On

A quotation from Barthes does not automatically carry
the day.   —David Bordwell[45]

[M]y taste for quotation, which I have always kept. Why re-
proach us for it? People, in life, quote what pleases them.
We have therefore the right to quote what pleases us.
                                —Jean-Luc Godard[46]

In "Lowering the Stakes" Bordwell makes the familiar Kuhnian argument that knowledge depends on a disciplinary consensus that demarcates a terrain. Film studies' purely theoretical dimension Bordwell regards as equivalent to Kuhn's periods of "philosophizing"—a symptom of a field's stalled distress. The essay's opening is worth quoting at length:

One indication of the vigor of film study in the 1970s was the speed with which theorists moved to confront and assimilate insights from other disciplines. Every few months, it seemed, literary theory, semiology, feminism, linguistics, marxism, psychoanalysis, and anthropology furnished provocative new ideas. One result of this trend was a tendency to frame ever more totalized accounts of cinema. The more concepts that one borrowed from such a range of ideas, the more colossal became the domain of film theory and the more general and abstract became the construct that theorists sought to build. At a certain point, a theory of the cinema blurred indistinguishably into theories of the psyche, of the human subject, of the social formation, of history and of communication. By the early 1980s, film research came to resemble a reckless poker game in which the ante was constantly rising. A decent theory of cinema, it seemed, would have to include an abstract explanation of everything that might ever have impinged upon or been presupposed by any cinematic phenomenon.

It is plain, I hope, that I am not denying the need for a theory of cinema to ground itself explicitly in a wider conceptual domain. But the analysis of any form of intellectual inquiry must distinguish among three different things: the enabling presuppositions; the logical structure of the theory; and the method whereby the theory is constructed, tested, and criticized. The expansionism of recent theory is partly traceable to the attempt to insert every conceivable presupposition into the theory.

This not only weakens the logical structure of the theory; it postpones specific formulations of methods. More particularly, the totalized theories of recent years have been largely content to reshuffle fixed concepts without confronting them with concrete particulars. . . . There comes a point where a theoretical formulation must not simply cite presuppositions and select privileged instances but test itself against a body of detailed evidence.

It is in this spirit that I suggest that there is value in more smallscale theorizing and that Russian Formalist literary criticism can help us accomplish it. . . .

At this point in the history of film study, we are best served by framing limited questions. I would add that answering these questions requires an interplay between abstract propositions and concrete bodies of evidence—an interplay which Russian Formalism, in its most promising guises, promotes. (5–7)

The most striking thing about Bordwell's argument is how much it resembles Comte's rationale for positivism. Structurally, in fact, the two are identical, with the inefficiency of disorder (blamed on epistemological competition) contrasted with the benefits of stability (promised by philosophical consensus). In calling for a suspension of film-study-as-revolutionary-science for the sake of a normal-science consolidation around a single paradigm (which, as was the case with Comte, happens to be his own), Bordwell implicitly reaffirms Comte's insistence that knowledge depends on suppression. Knowledge begins, in other words, only by putting an end to theory proliferation, a move (making a killing?) that *stakes out* a terrain, a regime of law and order where policing becomes possible.

A modest, good-humored essay, "Lowering the Stakes" nevertheless has things in common with Frederick Crews's polemic, "The Grand Academy of Theory": an impatience with nonapplied theorizing, a faith in Baconian hypothesis testing, a belief in specialization.[47] Indeed, Bordwell's complaint that film studies' infatuation with theory impedes knowledge about particular movies finds its exact echo in Crews:

Take, for example, the use of imported theory in American academic film studies, which are now dominated by a pugnacious clique that regards itself as at once Lacanian, Marxist, and feminist. Its journals, which are as fawning toward radical system builders as they are implacable toward the patriarchal-capitalist order, allow little room amid the manifestoes for discussion of actual movies. ("The Grand Academy of Theory," 173)

This subordination of theory to practical criticism, when coupled with Bordwell's frequent insistence on "primary" sources (see *CHC* and the attack on Burch) implies this position's metaphysical dimension, precisely the one challenged by Benjamin's "Work of Art in the Age of Mechanical Reproduction." In Bordwell's view, "truth" diminishes as we move away from the text itself: thus, while "primary" sources contemporary with a particular filmmaking mode (e.g., Hollywood's trade, technical, and union journals) are relatively trustworthy, later historical interpretations are not. Citing Burch's "lack of interest in the basic research necessary for any historian," Bordwell argues that Burch

seems content to rely on previous historians rather than tackle the huge amount of primary data that actually exists on the early cinema. In a recently published article, "Charles Baudelaire Versus Doctor Frankenstein," Burch footnotes Jacques Deslandes' history of early world cinema, Ceram's *Archaeology of the Cinema,* books on Muybridge and Lumière, and a few primary sources— Marey's works on animal movement, an 1894 *Century Magazine* interview with Edison. These last citations are exceptions in Burch's works; he seldom uses primary material and never cites contemporary trade papers or the numerous books and popular journal articles of the silent period.[48]

Although CHC repeatedly insists on its non-*auteurist* approach, on the need to look at Hollywood's *langue* and not its *parole,* the persistent discrediting of "secondary" commentary serves to reinscribe the hierarchy of "auratic" presence that made *auteurism,* for all its radical posturings, a conservative, late-romantic movement.[49]

The Bordwell regime, with "Lowering the Stakes" as its charter, was implemented with an intellectual *blitzkrieg* in which, by a sudden outpouring of important work, one seizes a field for a particular theoretical approach. (Derrida's 1967 comes to mind, and with it, the understanding that to effect such a *coup,* one must produce work perceived by its designated community as "first-rate.") Bordwell, who before 1985 had published steadily but modestly, then issued within the span of a dozen years seven books. These volumes all function as part of the same project: to install formalism as the dominant paradigm in film studies (a field for which Bordwell, perhaps significantly, prefers the singular, "film *study*").

What can we say about the Bordwell regime of knowledge? First, given its subject (the Classical Hollywood Cinema), it is curiously blind to its own unquestioning participation in our culture's hegemonic arrangements between truth and power. In *CHC,* BST lay bare how a particular mode of communication, historically constituted, came to appear natural and inevitable. They have not chosen to examine similarly their own "scientific" methodologies. Presumably following Brecht's and Benjamin's point that a producer should bequeath an improved apparatus, Foucault once insisted that

the essential political problem for the intellectual is not to criticize the ideological contents supposedly linked to science, or to ensure that his own scientific practice is accompanied by a correct ideology, but to ascertain the possibility of constituting a new politics of truth. The problem is not changing people's consciousness—or what's in their heads—but the political, economic, institutional regime of the production of truth.[50]

While Surrealism obviously influenced the style of Foucault's own baroque histories, his emphasis on the knowledge-politics connection derives from French neoclassicism, whose leaders consistently urged the implementation of Enlightenment ideas. Historically, classicism has proved more worldly than the baroque, perhaps because its own practical self-image encourages intervention in the administrative matters that the baroque disregards. Bordwell's "Lowering the Stakes," an explicit attempt to direct an institution's future, is thus a move as characteristically classical as Comte's *Cours de Philosophie Positive*. At this point, however, the analysis becomes confused. For all of classicism's typical complaints against the baroque's apolitical hedonism (see contemporary critiques of postmodernism), the baroque obviously maintains its own investment in a particular social vision, albeit a tacit one. Ultimately, therefore, classicism's *explicitness* is what distinguishes it from the baroque, which, like revolutionary science (pure research), seems always to be working, at best, by indirection.

With this opposition in mind, let us not argue with what BST have accomplished. Instead, let us be grateful for the information they have given and say that, offering us a *stake*, a *share* in their enterprise, they have left it to us to ask these questions:

QUESTION 1: CAN KNOWLEDGE BENEFIT FROM
PROLONGING A FIELD'S REVOLUTIONARY MOMENTS?

Among the principal theories of knowledge, *The Structure of Scientific Revolutions* most prominently represents the proposition that knowledge *requires* the suspension of revolutionary moments of doubt, self-scrutiny, and searching. Accepting rationalization and the division of labor, picturing happy specialists devoted to "problem solving," *The Structure* reflects at least the stereotype of the period of its conception, the 1950s. Kuhn, of course, was not just another organization man; he left himself a way out with the concept of "the essential tension," the Lévi-Straussian opposition of tradition and innovation on which science presumably turned.[51] An important study could be done of *The Structure*'s own history, which has both confirmed and refuted the book's argument. For while *The Structure* itself certainly set a paradigm for subsequent workers (among them Kuhn himself), the book also forms part of a knowledge explosion in the humanities (structuralism, semiotics, poststructuralism, etc.) that, far from restricting itself to "mopping up," has in fact *discredited* normal science, at least as a pursuit worthy of the most advanced researchers.[52]

At its worst, such discrediting (dismissed by Crews as self-indulgent "apriorism") inhibits that commitment to a research program on which knowledge depends. At its best, however, contemporary theory's innovative restlessness has exposed Kuhn's Darwinian fatalism that the creative breakthroughs *on which everything depends* simply occur as they occur, as indifferent to solicitation as biological variation. By definition, Kuhn's vision cannot address the basic question confronting the humanities: How do we arrange a climate that will encourage the profitable mutations we call "creativity"? In the post-Cartesian world, whose institutions are heavily weighted toward the teaching and rewarding of analysis, the notion of the *inventio,* a creativity machine, has been largely abandoned.[53] (The Surrealist and Oulipo games stand as noticeable exceptions.[54]) We analyze creativity and its products, but we have no idea how to stimulate it. And on this point, Kuhn is of no help.

Kuhn's great opponent Paul Feyerabend, however, is. If *The Structure* makes the case for consolidation and discipline, *Against Method* represents proliferation and hedonism. Knowledge advances, according to Feyerabend, when we "keep our options open" and do "not restrict ourselves in advance."[55] Indeed, forced conformity to a paradigm is counterproductive, for it "inhibit[s] intuitions" and constrains the imagination (19); "it leads to a deterioration of intellectual capabilities" (45). Worse, conformity is no fun; it drains the improvisatory pleasure out of knowledge, redefining it as industrial work.[56] Against this sterilization, Feyerabend offers his famous formulation: "there is only *one* principle that can be defended under *all* circumstances and in *all* stages of human development. It is the principle: *anything goes*" (28). Another *stake:* knowledge as a *gamble.*

Even though we are not accustomed to thinking of it in this way, the production of knowledge always puts something at risk. One summer, for example, I spent two weeks teaching in a Lilly Foundation workshop that annually convenes four-person teams from twenty to twenty-five colleges to talk about problems in the humanities: a gamble (of time and money) that something more than commonplaces will arise, that some student's education (and life) will benefit. What are the odds? Feyerabend urges us to gamble more recklessly: by ignoring disciplinary boundaries, by listening to "outsiders" or even dilettantes,[57] by suspecting experts, and, in particular, by adapting for research the methods of the twentieth century's avant-garde arts and nontraditional sciences. "*We need a dream-world,*" Feyerabend writes, "*in order to discover the features of the real world we think we inhabit*"[58]; and for that alternative, astrology and Dada may prove more useful than science would lead us to believe. If these propositions seem risky, Roger Shattuck has reminded us that our civilization has always gambled, if only homeopathically:

Sade, Holderlin, Nerval, Nietzsche, and Artaud were at some point certified by the culture as criminal or pathological; yet their lives and their work have not been cast out of the Republic of Letters. Quite the contrary; we carefully preserve their biographical and literary remains in the usually unstated belief that their strain may yield a valuable inoculation against dangerous ideas, including some of their own. This homeopathic faith justifying liberalism of mind and opposing Plato's banishment of poets probably represents the most exciting risk Western culture has taken.

But how can we tell if we are preserving a strain too virulent to serve as vaccination?[59]

The answer is, we cannot; and Feyerabend welcomes the uncertainty. He would surely regard the homeopathic metaphor, with its emphasis on risk, as the negative version of his brief for proliferation. To Feyerabend, revolutionary moments, whatever the stakes, exhilarate (remember Wordsworth's account of experiencing the French Revolution: "Bliss was it in that dawn to be alive"); it is the dogmatism that follows, the staking out, the burning of heretics (at the stake) that are deadly. An institution that refuses to gamble, Lyotard suggests, destroys a major source of new knowledge; it submits itself to unquestioned standards of legitimation that "function to filter discursive potentials, interrupting possible connections in the communication network." The solution:

We know today that the limits the institution imposes on potential language "moves" are never established once and for all (even if they have been formally defined). Rather the limits are themselves *the stakes* and provisional results of language strategies, within the institution and without. . . . the boundaries only stabilize when they cease to be *stakes* in the game.[60]

How does this debate apply to film studies in general, and to Bordwell's Kuhnian proposals for consolidation around the formalist paradigm in particular? We can start to answer this question by noting that from its inception in this country, film studies has been a curiosity: a "discipline" practiced largely by untrained, uncertified amateurs, frequently other fields' malcontents. Only recently have academic film studies positions been filled by graduates of organized cinema programs. This historically low level of expertise has inevitably spurred the discipline's most rigorous practitioners to call for the paradigm consensus and normal science that Kuhn regards as the *sine qua non* of "genuine knowledge." Bordwell's "Lowering the Stakes" obviously participates in this impulse toward professionalization. But as a response to what he apparently regards as film studies' "pre-paradigmatic" state, Bordwell's proposals come too late. For in decrying current film scholars' mechanical, uncritical deployment of received theories and terminology, Bordwell is in fact describing an already entrenched *normal science*, an activity that, according to Feyerabend, depletes even its practitioners' vocabularies.[61] Certainly a visit to almost any academic conference nowadays—but especially those on film—will reveal how much the *fatigue* we have come to expect from media exploitation, saturation, and recuperation now affects ideas. And why not? Over a century ago, Marx taught us that ideas were a commodity like any other; and Nietzsche, that they were fashion and thus subject to whim and massification. In an academic climate that pressures even its graduate students to publish in order to be employable, the inevitable happens: a catchy, malleable idea like Lacan's "mirror stage" suddenly crops up as the basis for hundreds of articles and conference papers (mostly on individual movies: practical criticism dies hard), only to be replaced by a new fad, the race/class/gender template.

What is the answer to this impasse at which the humanities as a whole find themselves? "These are the days," Walter Benjamin once wrote, in advice that applies to us, "when no one should rely unduly on his 'competence.' Strength lies in improvisation. All the decisive blows are struck left-handed."[62] In other words, while we should retain normal science, we must become more tolerant of the baroque: the *surprising,* the *strange,* even the *preposterous gag,* which, as Barthes saw, blocks trivializing recuperations and may ultimately lead to new knowledge.[63] Gregory Ulmer has specifically praised "the theory joke,"[64] whose prototypes are Duchamp's readymades (about which people have not been able to stop talking for nearly a century), but, in fact, all radically new knowledge *at first seems like a joke* (think of Darwin and the monkeys). As Freud saw, the joke is a denial that also functions as a means of access, a channel capable of being confronted directly.

Against Method's arguments for sustaining a field's revolutionary moments come mainly in the guise of attacks on normal science; Feyerabend never really tells us how to construct a revolutionary practice. In poststructuralism, however, we have precisely a model for such an activity, a new methodology of knowledge whose principles are the following:

A) *"Yield the initiative to words."* Of poststructuralism's leading figures, the one most successful in sustaining a revolutionary disposition toward knowledge was Roland Barthes. Not surprisingly, his autobiography is the most explicit account we have of how such thinking works. Throughout his career, Barthes emphasized his status as "an amateur" of learning, a word chosen first for its connotation of "non-specialist" (Barthes often pointed to his lack of "the right degrees"[65]), but also for its etymological meaning of "lover." Here is the crucial passage:

La machine de l'écriture—The writing machine

Around 1963 (apropos of La Bruyere in *Critical Essays*) he worked up a great enthusiasm for the *metaphor/metonymy* opposition (though it had been familiar to him already, ever since his conversations with G. in 1950). Like a magician's wand, the concept, especially if it is coupled, raises a possibility of writing: here, he said, lies the power of saying something.

Hence the work proceeds by conceptual infatuations, successive enthusiasms, perishable manias. Discourse advances by little fates, by amorous fits. (*Roland Barthes,* 110)

What does this strategy entail? It asks only that we allow ourselves to venture in directions toward which certain words vaguely point, words that, for some as-yet-unaccountable reason, captivate us and provide what Barthes calls *"a flush of pleasure"* (103). While this procedure may seem bizarre (or baroque), it conforms to an increasingly widespread understanding that knowledge develops differently from how we have previously imagined. Recently, scholars from several disciplines have converged on the notion that Barthes formulated as an autobiographical trait: *"I have ideas on the level of language"* (85). Thus, Feyerabend insists that the most important scientific thinking begins not with ideas, but with words that become appealing:

It is often taken for granted that a clear and distinct understanding of new ideas precedes, and should precede, their formulation and institutional expression. (An investigation starts with a problem, says Popper.) *First,* we have an idea, or a problem, *then* we act, *i.e.,* either speak, or build, or destroy. Yet this is certainly not the way in which small children develop. They use words, they combine them, they play with them, until they grasp a meaning that has so far been beyond their reach. And the initial playful activity is an essential prerequisite of the final act of understanding. There is no reason why this mechanism should cease to function in the adult.[66]

For some reason, which we do not yet fully understand, a particular phrase or vocabulary can reanimate a whole domain. Such "constitutive" words do not simply explain in colorful imagery something already known (the purpose of "exegetical" or "pedagogical" metaphors); rather they "suggest strategies for future research," "put us on the track" of what will become a redefined normal science.[67] Indeed, as Richard Boyd maintains, "the utility of these metaphors in theory change crucially depends upon [their] open-endedness." (357)

Contrary, then, to Bordwell's complaints about the "[r]eliance on vaporous formulas rather than on explicitly constructed concepts and propositions,"[68] this constitutive vocabulary's inchoateness should not count against it; in fact, its very imprecision fosters a "learning disposition," that impulse toward knowledge that originates in vaguely motivated but urgent desire.[69] As Dan Sperber points out, for someone intrigued by a remark such as Lacan's famous "The unconscious is structured like a language,"

[T]he problem . . . is not to validate or invalidate a statement. He knows that [it] expresses a valid statement, but he does not know which one. Thus, he searches. Doing so, his mind opens itself to a whole series of problems, certain possibilities appear, certain relationships impose themselves. He has therefore not necessarily wasted his time in taking [the statement] as valid. By taking it in quotes, he opens it to interpretation, he treats it symbolically.[70]

Poststructuralism has discovered that Mallarmé's famous advice to poets, "Yield the initiative to words," is the basis for cognitive research as well. From this perspective, even apparently classical knowledge systems begin to seem baroque. What, after all, are the disciplines of psychoanalysis and biology except institutions developed to pursue the words "the unconscious" and "natural selection"? Film studies, too, has organized itself around those figures or schools offering the most tantalizing vocabularies: "*auteur*" (the *Cahiers du Cinéma* critics), "montage" (Eisenstein), photography as a "tracing" of reality and the screen as a "window" (Bazin), the cinema as "a grammar" (Metz), "the institutional mode of representation" (Burch).[71] Even Godard's uncompromisingly cryptic "A dolly shot is a moral statement" has prompted a sustained research tradition investigating the inferred form-ideology connection.[72]

Such "constitutive" words or phrases are precisely not yet ideas, but rather maps for which the territory must be, not found, but invented; incomplete allegories, clues (Sherlock Holmes's dog that does nothing in the nighttime), hermeneutic enigmas, what Walter Benjamin called "the rumor about true things."[73] *Roland Barthes* offers several names for these research-generating terms: "*mots-valeurs*," "fashion words," "mana-words," "color-words"[74] (where the analogy is to exotic colors like "celadon green" that outline a "kind of generic region within which the exact, special effect of the color is unforeseeable; the name is then the promise of a pleasure, the program of an operation" [129]). The word, as Barthes says, "transports me because of the notion that *I am going to do something with it*" (129). Its mysteriousness, far from being a defect, enhances its power to seduce, for such words are fetishes, swiveling back and forth between the desire to know and the desire to remain ignorant: "[transitional words] are of uncertain status; actually it is a kind of absence of the object, of meaning that they *stage*" (130).

With major figures, the researcher's individual fetishes coincide with (or lead) a whole discourse. Thus, while intending to name only the words that occasioned his own work, Barthes in fact revealed how much his interests became a generation's: "the imaginary," "history," "mythology," "the natural," "textuality," "the signifier," "*jouissance*," "the writerly," "the body," etc. We should remember, however, that in following language's lead, Barthes was not a special case. Nor should we dismiss the research directions sponsored by such research words when the passing of time exposes their creator's inconsistencies or factual mistakes. Those who formulate a discipline's research words become what Foucault called "founders of discursivity," "unique in that they are not just the authors of their works. They have produced something else: the possibilities and the rules for the formation of other texts."[75] In fact, such inventiveness necessarily contemplates the very investigations that will eventually uncover its lapses.[76] As Barthes maintained, for example, Michelet may have gotten some facts wrong, but he invented French history.[77] Thus, to the extent that Noël Burch's phrase "the Institutional Mode of Representation" stimulated the writing of *CHC* (and an enormous body of other work besides), Bordwell and Thompson are ungrateful to dismiss him for having erred on the date for studio lighting's implementation.

Such criticism issues from a literal-mindedness discarded by the new revolutionary tactics. The experimental researcher, a gambler, refuses to be bound by a heuristic vocabulary's original meaning. Indeed, our epoch has invented a new type of the "founder of discursivity": the collagist who does not coin his own terms but who grafts (and thereby remotivates) ones already available. Walter Benjamin, who saw in the gambler the representative modern man and in collage the potential modern history, recognized early that photography and film are collage machines, endlessly recombining fragments detached from their previous contexts.[78] Barthes frankly admitted his own similar disloyalty to prior meanings:

[O]ne steals a language, though without wishing to apply it to the end: impossible to say: this is denotation, this connotation, or: this passage is readerly, this writerly, etc., the opposition is *struck* (like a coinage), but one does not seek to *honor* it. Then what good is it? Quite simply, it serves to say something: it is necessary to posit a paradigm in order to produce a meaning and then be able to divert, to alter it. (92)

In this way, "one plays at science, one puts it in the picture—like a piece in a collage" (100), or, even more baldly,

words are shifted, systems communicate, modernity is tried (the way one tries all the push buttons on a radio one doesn't know how to work), but the intertext thereby created is literally *superficial.* . . . one cannot at one and the same time desire every word and take it to its conclusion. . . . (74)

While characteristically postmodern, this opportunistic use of other disciplines' vocabularies has a long history. Think of Darwin's borrowing Herbert Spencer's phrase "survival of the fittest" and the migrations of the words "censorship" and "overdetermination" between psychoanalysis and politics. This recombinatory strategy avoids fixed positions (among Barthes's "Dislikes" was "fidelity" [117]): "you cannot get to the heart of a refrain"; Barthes advises, "you can only substitute another one for it" (127). The result is that Barthes "pays his visits, i.e., his respects to vocabularies," but he dispenses with "following to its conclusion the system of which [they are] the signifier" (74). He does not settle; he *pulls up stakes* and moves on, imitating the "nomad thought" of Nietzsche.[79]

As a research strategy, the free appropriation and mixing of other disciplines' terminologies serve the researcher as an *inventio,* a means of thinking the unexpected. Bordwell himself is not averse to this move, although except for the musicological vocabulary he often borrows from Leonard Meyer (e.g., "trended change"), he seldom wanders into fields more distant than literary criticism. (Of course, he, like everyone else—including me—raids Thomas Kuhn.) If there is a complaint to be made against Bordwell, then, it is that he is too modest. As one of the most brilliant persons working in American film studies, he could be coining the research words for the next generation. Instead, his insistence on empirically testing carefully framed hypotheses commits him to caution and a retreat from revolutionary science. In our current situation, at the end of a particular classicism, does this position have any validity? Of course. Although prolonging film studies' revolutionary moment would certainly open up unanticipated zones of possibility, we need normal scholarship to explore implications of a field's most striking ideas. In that sense, *CHC* provides, in effect, a long footnote refining Noël Burch's pioneering work on the transition from "primitive" to "classical" cinema. The question is only whether Bordwell might be engaged in something different.[80] What that "something different" might entail is the second principle of poststructuralist knowledge.

B) *The shift from coverage to concept formation.* "We are entering," Barthes observed in 1966, "a *general crisis of commentary,* perhaps as important as that which marked . . . the transition from the Middle Ages to the Renaissance."[81] As Barthes intuited, this crisis (which continues) first turned on the contested issue of clarity. With its self-proclaimed commitment to "objectivity" and "truth," classicism has normally championed a transparent style, supposedly allowing an uninflected view of its given "subject." The very presence, however, of the preceding sentence's quotation marks suggests the influence of the baroque, which has consistently (albeit indirectly) challenged naturalized conceptions of a neutral language. The baroque delight in style, elegance, novelty, surface, and complexity begins in mannerism[82] and flowers again in poststructuralism's word play, aestheticization, neologisms, catachreses, and esoterica— all predictably denounced by classicists.[83] Poststructuralism's main contribution to what Richard Rorty calls "the edifying tradition" consists of converting these strategies from tools of criticism into instruments of knowledge.[84]

In doing so, poststructuralism has provoked classicism's second line of defense, the demand for coverage. Surprising best-sellers, Allan Bloom's *Closing of the American Mind* and E. D. Hirsch, Jr.'s *Cultural Literacy* (with its significant subtitle, *What Every American Needs to Know*) both characterize as inadequate any educational system not devoting most of its time to transmitting what Hirsch calls "the elements of our shared culture" (132). When philosophically expressed, this position has obvious antecedents in Matthew Arnold and Samuel Johnson, not to mention Bloom's main source, *The Republic.* More immediately, however, it reflects the practical anxiety of teachers giving fourteen-week courses such as "World Literature from 1715 to the Present" and worrying about how to "get it all in." While that concern seems more or less realistic, the problem becomes clearer when academics feel just as bothered about having "only" a semester to cover "all" of Pope. As academic disciplines grow more specialized, as increasing competition fosters more articles and books, as electronic technology circulates this flood of information ever more rapidly and widely, the best response sometimes seems to be that of my colleague, who, when a fellow teacher complained about a six-week summer lit survey, commiserated, "I can never figure out how to fill up those last two weeks either."

The postmodern problem is the reverse of the Middle Ages': not too little information, but too much. As a partial cure, poststructuralism has developed a freer relationship to its objects of study, one that replaces superfluous commentary with demonstrations of concept formation. The strangeness of these texts results precisely from their rejecting the norms for "secondary" literature: someone who goes to Derrida's *Spurs,* for example, expecting another reading of Nietzsche, will be scandalized by what he or she finds—as Raymond Picard was by Barthes's *On Racine.* Such books are less about their tutor texts than occasioned by them. Instead of telling us what their objects of study mean, they show us how we might use them to think.

Derrida, in particular, has repeatedly demonstrated how tracking the literal level of signification can serve as a means of concept formation. In the signature effect (e.g., *Signéponge*), the research pun, and the interdisciplinary homonym (the place where two or more fields converge at a single set of terms; see *Glas*'s discussion of "*gênet,*" botany, and the "flowers" of rhetoric), we have strange, apparently preposterous tactics for confronting the demoralizing oversupply of information. Here are artificial machines, whose capacities for invention complement the computer's for normal science: both types shuttle fluently among multiple symbolic systems. Gregory Ulmer has shown how such a machine might work. After quoting Eisenstein's remarks about Ivan the

Terrible (a god "invented out of whole cloth," "but *as the creator of the linen trade,* the Czar who enriched and strengthened Russia's economic position, he becomes a more interesting figure"), Ulmer continues:

> Ivan [Eisenstein's film *Ivan the Terrible*], that is, may be read as another gods sequence [resembling the one in Eisenstein's *October*], demystifying a legend if not a religion. More importantly, the "god" being demystified, at the level of inner speech, at least, may not be Ivan but Lenin himself (his cult of personality fostered by Stalin), for the verbal image working here is the pun association Lenin with linen (by antonomasia). The pun is English, of course, but then Eisenstein was fluent in English. . . . The allusion links Lenin's signature with Marx in that one of the principal examples of the theory of the commodity in *Capital* is the linen trade in England.[85]

Whatever this paragraph is, it is *not* an argument in the traditional sense (despite its parodic use of logical transitions such as "for") and certainly *not* an argument one might expect to encounter at a regular film studies conference. Indeed, its rationale involves precisely its unpredictability:

> If traditional pedagogy attempted a transparent, univocal transmission of a body of information, understood as the contents or signifieds of a discipline, an open pedagogy concerns itself with information as it is understood in General Systems Theory, cybernetics, and the like, defined in terms of the probability or improbability of a message within a rule-governed system. The more probable (banal) the message, the less information it conveys. "Information" here is statistical, referring not to what one says but to what one *could* say. . . . The pun or homophone acquires a new status with respect to the new sensibility, attuned no longer to the expectations of cause and effect, the logic of the excluded middle, but to the pleasure of surprise, in that homophones represent "the bridge of least motivation," thus generating the greatest "information." (*Applied Grammatology*, 308–309)

As a knowledge strategy, the pursuit of the signifier maintains the revolutionary moment: *one cannot predict where it will lead.* Further, it displaces the endlessly vexed problem of specialization by leaving intact the various disciplines, only to find among them connections we have not learned to expect. It is a device for *rechanneling* our flows of information, for burning in new circuits, so that we might escape the characteristically modern malaise that regards as futile discussion of even our most important issues: nuclear energy, abortion rights, capital punishment, feminism vs. the family, pornography and censorship.[86] Within film studies, the list expands daily: the position of the subject, suture, mass media and ideology, etc. If these devices enable us to think in any new ways about such realistically critical problems, then the gamble, the stake, will have paid off.

The tactic I have been describing starts from the premise that "information" (or "knowledge") will be cybernetically redefined as *the unpredictable.* In doing so, it symptomizes what Hauser called the baroque's "impulse towards the unrestrained and the arbitrary" (*The Social History of Art,* 177). In fact, however, Derrida's work mixes chance with method by subjecting the most fruitful homonymic accidents to rigorous investigation.[87] The prototypes for this procedure are the Surrealist writing experiments (decalcomania, the exquisite corpse, "How to Write False Novels"), a fact suggesting that postmodernism may best be understood as a new attitude toward the avant-garde arts. That branch of the humanities, previously marginalized by modernism, is reconceived as the equivalent of science's pure research, a field of experimental work whose devices prove capable of knowledge.[88]

In an essay discussing what counts as literary criticism, Jonathan Culler has used "The Three Little Pigs" to suggest that

almost every *proper* question, such as "what happened next?" will be critically less productive (less productive of critical discourse we find worth reading) than marginally improper questions, such as "why three little pigs?"[89]

The avant-garde is a source of "improper questions," new concepts that enable us to jump tracks worn out from overuse. We have in older libraries' card catalogues a concrete image of research's routinization: along the well-traveled paths (an author's name, an obvious subject heading), the cards are bent, smudged, exhausted. Nearly twenty years ago, Barthes observed that standardization overtakes even the most radical ideas, which then become less the instigators of research than "cathechistic declaration," the new *doxa.*[90] Now, when ideas spread as fast as hairstyles, poststructuralism's emphasis on concept formation makes even more sense.

Why do some concepts (e.g., "deconstruction," "the Imaginary") catch on and spread throughout a discipline? Using an analogy to epidemiology, Dan Sperber has proposed that certain cultural formulations are "contagious," and as such reveal the "infected" group's particular susceptibilities. The extraordinary success of Derridean terminology should, therefore, tell us something about American humanities departments.[91] In fact, however, academic institutions may not be unique; like other population groups, they are affected by those mechanisms of publicity charged with fostering desire. If so, then poststructuralism's second wave (postpoststructuralism?) may well look to advertising and market research for ideas about making new concepts "catching." Lacan's teaching success, for example, suggests that the advertising staples "mystification" and "celebrity" can function pedagogically. Another obvious

possibility is "High Concept," a phrase associated with Hollywood's preference for movies packaged around an easily marketed story line or actor (e.g.,
Eddie Murphy as an African prince looking for an American bride): in other
words, a way of attracting an audience. What more appropriate goal could exist for teachers, writers, artists? The most important issue for contemporary
intellectuals is whether strategies such as "High Concept" (originating in, and
supposedly corrupted by, "enemy" areas such as business, the military, and
propaganda) can be remotivated for other purposes. If such collusive refunc-
tioning of commercial procedures amounts to the basis of postmodernism
(think of Andy Warhol), then its academic equivalent might help establish a
pedagogy adequate to our own cultural moment.

Whether or not to prolong a discipline's revolutionary moments is an issue for all the arts and sciences. The next question prompted by *CHC* involves
the particular situation of film studies.

QUESTION 2: IF FILM STUDIES MUST CONSOLIDATE AROUND A PARADIGM, IS FORMALISM THE ONE BEST SATISFYING OUR NEEDS?

As I have mentioned earlier, Bordwell's "Lowering the Stakes" proposes at
least a preliminary coordination of research, to be implemented by at least a
temporary suspension of "Big Theory" for the smaller, but presumably more
verifiable, gains afforded by Russian Formalism. Almost certainly, the Comtean assumptions of Bordwell's essay predispose him to some kind of formalism, since, as I have argued, positivism itself is formalistic. Nevertheless, despite the appealing reasonableness of "Lowering the Stakes" (not to mention
of Comte, one of philosophy's most seductive thinkers), the answer to question 2 depends first on the definition of "formalism."

Since its American institutionalization in the 1960s, film studies has always been a permeable field, enmeshed in other disciplines in a way that Bordwell apparently regards as dissipative. The interdisciplinary nature of film
studies, however, was an attempt to represent the cinema's own massive overdetermination, its implication (as a commercial, technologically based mass-
medium) in multiple discourses. In particular, film scholars who had emi-
grated from literature programs quickly saw that the relative autonomy that
they had (falsely) attributed to "high art" was obviously unjustifiable with
something such as *Casablanca:* topical (at least in its own time), moneymak-
ing, sentimental. And, too, practical criticism's standard thematic analyses,
geared to the subtly ironic density of "serious" fiction, yielded only plati-
tudes when applied to the popular cinema, which traded on the equally dense,
but more obvious, intertextuality that *S/Z* eventually identified as underpin-
ning all popular narratives. The movies, in Christian Metz's formulation, were
"hard to explain because they were easy to understand."

Struggling to retain the traditional methodologies authorized by "high art," American film studies began by clustering around those (chiefly European) filmmakers whose work most resembled (or could be *made* to resemble) "literature": Antonioni, Resnais, De Sica, Fellini, Rossellini, Bresson, and, above all, Bergman. The resulting early criticism of Bergman in particular constitutes a record of the discipline's avoidance of the problems posed not by "film" (in John Simon's famous, and middlebrow, distinction) but by "the movies." Sooner or later, however, film studies had to come to terms with its own subject matter, and ultimately the discipline's history demonstrates the ecological principle: a system (in this case, the academy) accepting a newly introduced element cannot stay the same and survive. The cinema, in short, demanded new critical approaches. Some of the standard literary methods endured (*CHC* often uses them profitably), but new ones also appeared. Now a mature discipline, cinema studies suddenly finds itself in literature's shoes, confronted by television, which overlaps with film but also poses different questions.

The young discipline of film studies proved relentlessly assimilative, borrowing methodologies from established fields: anthropology, political science, sociology, economics, etc. In its heyday, it both prompted and benefited from the generalized erosion of strict academic boundaries and canons. Further, what Bordwell calls "the vigor of film study in the 1970s" stemmed from the cinema's capacity (unmatched before television) to pose dramatically what have become the two central problematics of postmodernism—the volatility of signs and the collapse of the high art/mass culture distinction—topics whose very natures forestall attempts to restrict the scope of inquiry. We can begin to sense formalism's inadequacy for our situation by acknowledging this basic fact of the postmodernist experience: the (art) object no longer controls our reading of it. Or as Walter Benjamin says about allegory, one of postmodernism's preferred modes, "Any person, object, any relationship can mean absolutely anything else."[92]

This is not the place to venture a full-fledged definition of "postmodernism," but since the term is both recent and contested, I should at least say what I mean by it. I have in mind both a historical condition and a group of corresponding strategies (aesthetic and otherwise), remaining in force and intensifying since their origins in mid-nineteenth-century Paris, the period when mechanically reproduced art (photographs, books, lithographs) and the attendant mass culture first challenged the supremacy of traditional aesthetics. If the modernist response was to retreat from this scene (by using difficulty to protect works from mass appropriation; see Mallarmé), the postmodernist one was to settle within it, experimenting with the possibilities afforded by its structures in a deadpan, complicitous merger of criticism and profiteering for which dandyism (a critique of consumerism dependent on shopping) is the prototype (see Warhol).

I can clarify this probably cryptic definition with a specific example: the case of Douglas Sirk. Of Danish extraction, he settled in Germany, working in the theater until 1934, when he began making films at UFA, the largest German studio. He left three years later, by which time his vaguely leftist credentials had begun to cause him trouble. Settling in the United States in 1939, he languished at Warner Brothers and Columbia before catching on at Universal, where he made the five movies on which his reputation rests: *Magnificent Obsession* (1952), *All That Heaven Allows* (1955), *Written on the Wind* (1956), *Tarnished Angels* (1957), and *Imitation of Life* (1959). This work is of a piece: big-budget, commercially successful (except for *Tarnished Angels*) melodramas, starring Rock Hudson (except for *Imitation*). At their release, they received no critical attention; like most Hollywood product, they did their job—they entertained, made money, and were forgotten.

In the late 1960s, however, having retired to Switzerland, Sirk began giving a series of interviews (starting with the *Cahiers du Cinéma* in 1967) that paid off in 1972 with the Edinburgh Film Festival's twenty-film retrospective and two books: *Douglas Sirk* and *Sirk on Sirk: Interviews with Jon Halliday*.[93] Sirk now claimed that his movies (which within ten years had dated remarkably, becoming camp reminders of an abandoned style) had, in fact, been subversive, critical, satirical parodies of American "bourgeois" values and Hollywood's taste for melodrama. As a move, this claim (this *stake*) extended Duchamp's readymades tactic, for Sirk had remotivated found objects that were his own work without modifying or "correcting" them in any way. (The closest comparison would be to Duchamp's remotivated Mona Lisa ["Shaved"], which leaves the original untouched but depends on Duchamp's previous modification, the goateed *L.H.O.O.Q.*)

Intentionally or not, Sirk had perfectly timed his play (his gamble). It was eagerly received by an Anglo-American film studies community flushed with two incompatible enthusiasms: *auteurism* and leftist ideology. Sirk provided a bridge between the two, as an *auteur* hero whose struggle against Hollywood's "repressive studio system" had involved sly criticisms of bourgeois ideology. That this "bourgeois ideology" rested above all on exactly the kind of individualism that *auteurism* assumed bothered no one. The Sirk boom was on, and analyses of his films flowered in journals and at conferences. By 1978, one film scholar could matter-of-factly refer to Sirk's "famous ironic subtext."[94]

Discussion of Sirk typically developed as hybrid-formalist analyses of what came to be known as "the Sirkian system," a set of distanciation devices that purportedly undermined his films' "illusionism" and thus their "apparent" ideological complacency. These devices, which were said to appear most prominently in the movies around which the Sirk boom formed (the Universal melodramas), came down to a penchant for stylizations not fully motivated by narrative: baroque color schemes, heavy-handed symbolization, obviously mannered acting, implausible plotting.[95] Classical Hollywood, of course, had forbidden such stylization, and to an audience that had internalized that film-making norm, these devices made Sirk's movies seem simply "bad" or, at best, dated. Even a Sirk admirer admitted the problem:

[W]e [film scholars participating in the Sirk boom] were always a bit uneasy there. Most audiences, after all, take these films straight. And even the "best" audiences are not always quite sure when they are seeing tackiness, or a criti-cism of it—an irony, or a mistake—a failure to achieve reality, or an intended unreality, an empty gesture or a comment on such gesturing.[96]

Theoretically, the Sirk boom depended on Anglo-American film studies' rediscovery of Brecht, whose work seemed to justify merging formalism with ideological criticism. Sirk (who had conveniently emerged out of the same Weimar theatrical scene) could be seen as practicing the "V-effect," with his movies becoming updated versions of "epic theater." One problem, however, remained: no one who had seen Sirk's movies in the 1950s had gotten their "real point." As supposedly political weapons, they had missed their mark, the most damning flaw possible from the perspective of Brecht, who had used popular forms (the ballad, the musical) to meet his audience half-way. Worse, in his debates with Lukács, Brecht had explicitly repudiated the formalism that assumes stable effects for aesthetic techniques.[97] That his own historically specific alienation tactics failed to work in a radically different context (1950s America) merely confirmed his point.

Because film studies clung to versions of formalist practical criticism, the Sirk phenomenon began to fade when it could not be rationalized in terms of the movies themselves. Indeed, the formalist attempts to do so duplicated those of art historians who had explained Duchamp's "Fountain" as an in-stance of traditional aesthetic "beauty." With Duchamp and Sirk, the formalist methodologies of modernism (with its faith in art's autonomy) reach their limits. As examples of postmodernism, Duchamp and Sirk represent the shift from work to textuality; postmodernism retains the notion of the art object but redefines it as a *site,* a crossroads traversed by communicative highways continuously rerouted by external, extratextual circumstances. Any method that attends *only* to the site will prove inadequate. Even a more general formal-ist poetics will not work. Could we, for example, itemize the properties of that class of texts most susceptible to Sirkian-styled remotivations? In 1964, Susan Sontag still thought we could, ironically saying of camp (the prototype of all drastic rereadings) that "not everything can be seen as Camp. It's not *all* in the eye of the beholder."[98]

But, of course, it *is*. What class of texts (or events) cannot be made over? High art? See Duchamp's versions of the Mona Lisa. Real historical tragedy? See *The Producers* or *To Be or Not to Be*, with their send-ups of Nazism.

Although Sirk claimed for himself the Adornoesque critical perspective of modernism, the Sirkian phenomenon (a different entity) signals the new situation we call postmodernism: (1) Sirk opportunistically seized on the instability, the *volatility* of his own signs—his movies began to mean different things; and (2) if it existed at all, his ideological critique had worked *in complicity* with dominant, even ideologically contaminated forms—melodrama, classical narrative, star vehicles, the commercial cinema, misogyny, etc. In his interviews, Sirk devalued the superficial level of his dated, forgotten works, converting them into allegories that, as Benjamin observes, "are, in the realm of thoughts, what ruins are in the realm of things."[99]

This allegorical venture forms a subset of postmodernism's characteristic fact: the limitless possibilities for *reading differently* that *S/Z* takes as its subject. In this situation (intensified by mass media's appropriative, disseminating power), the "network" (*S/Z*'s word) comprising the text is subjected to continuous rerouting, to *switching* in railroad parlance. (With the early railways, appearing so often in primitive American movies, the switchman redirected the track by *pulling up and moving a stake*.) Therein lies a new kind of cultural politics, what Eco calls "a semiotic guerrilla warfare":

[T]he gap between the transmitted and the received message is not only an aberration, which needs to be reduced—it can also be developed so as to broaden the receiver's freedom. In political activity it is not indispensable to change a given message: it would be enough (or, perhaps better) to change the attitude of the audience, so as to induce a different decoding of the message—or in order to isolate the intentions of the transmitter and thus to criticize them.[100]

Significantly, the disregard for the text itself, which this proposal assumes, was, from the start, part of Classical Hollywood's practice. Indeed, the studio system itself amounted to a mechanism for negotiating, influencing, or delimiting readings of the films produced there. Press releases, ads, posters, studio-sponsored fanzines, the star system, star bios, interviews, press leaks and plants, the Academy Awards, paid-for reviews—all sought to deemphasize the single movie's role in producing the desired reading: as a strategy, it hedged a studio's bets, spread responsibility for its releases' success or failure, protected its *stakes*. Aberrant decoding (such as Sirk's) enables individual readers (or groups: cf. feminist film scholars) to play this game as well, to remotivate Hollywood's product for other purposes.[101] Postmodernism recognizes, therefore, that meaning cannot be fully accounted for by formalism. Meaning becomes, in Brecht's word, an *apparatus* matter: production, distribution, and consumption all influence meaning, and the "encrustations" (reviews, gossip, economic situation of scholars, etc.) surrounding the text almost always dominate it.[102] We might say, for example, that the Sirk phenomenon's trajectory depended less on Sirk's movies than on an anxious academic community's eagerness for publishing *lebensraum* and its deference to European "intellectuals."

What does all of this have to do with Bordwell and *CHC*? We can start by saying that the narrow (but subtle) formalism Bordwell and Thompson have successfully applied to the "modernist cinema" (Dreyer, Eisenstein, Ozu) works less well with Hollywood. (Interestingly, some have objected that the readings of Ozu themselves constitute opportunistic remotivations of straightforward films.[103]) BST apparently realized the problem, for *CHC* marks a retreat (advance?) from the narrow formalism of "Lowering the Stakes," *The Films of Carl-Theodor Dreyer*, and Thompson's *Eisenstein's Ivan the Terrible: A Neoformalist Analysis*. *CHC*'s subject, of course, is a particular, institutionalized form and its historical evolution. But the explanation for that evolution has become increasingly difficult, as BST attempt to locate materialist causes for the fate of cinema's formal variations (e.g., cinemascope, color, deep focus). The Bordwell project announced in "Lowering the Stakes" ("smallscale theorizing" based on early formalism's "modest aims"[6–7]) has been partially abandoned, but the basic goal remains: "the explicit, detailed, and comprehensive analysis of norms" (14), here, the most dominant norm in the history of world cinema: Classical Hollywood. Despite its bulk, however, *CHC*'s approach reflects Bordwell's previous call for modesty: BST concentrate almost exclusively on the most immediate and local influences on style: developments in technology, the ambitions of technical specialists, the studios' specific economic constraints, etc. "Ideology" in *CHC* has been reduced to mean only commitment to narrative filmmaking. The larger ideological *stakes* of such filmmaking—its effects, its epistemic causes—are left unexplored because the book's methodology commits BST to risking only those hypotheses confirmable by empirical evidence. *CHC*'s predictability, then, derives from its refusal to bet. BST do not gamble with their *stakes* in film studies.

Here is my last question: Do we still need a discipline called "Film Studies"? *CHC* occurred at a juncture crucial to the humanities' future. Down one road lies the erosion of traditional specializations; down the other lies their reinforcement (under the sponsorship of William Bennett et al.). We do know that film studies as it currently defines itself has reinscribed the very modes of specialization against which it originally revolted. Do traditional fields inhibit knowledge? We cannot say for sure. To move away from them will represent a gamble, a *stake* risked and pulled up. For the moment, while our fields still exist, let us invoke another stake, a *share* we all have in each other's work and knowledge. As Barthes wrote of education,

When we say that knowledge must be shared, it is against death that this frontier is traced. *All for all.* . . . Knowledge, like delight, dies with each body. Whence the vital idea of a knowledge which circulates, which "mounts up" through different bodies, outside of books; *learn this for me, I'll learn that for you.*[104]

In writing *The Classical Hollywood Cinema*, Bordwell, Staiger, and Thompson have learned something for the rest of us.

4 Tracking

The Tin Pan Alley songs that have become what we know as "standards" typically derived from a specific songwriting process: the composer, responsible for the music, settled first on a melody and second on a harmonic accompaniment, consisting at this stage of usually no more than instructions regarding the chords that would inflect the vocal line in a particular way. The lyricist, presented with the completed music, would then set words to it, and the result would be something like "My Romance" (Rogers and Hart), "Someone to Watch over Me" (George and Ira Gershwin), or "Stardust" (Hoagy Carmichael and Mitchell Parish). Occasionally, of course, these jobs might be performed by the same person: George M. Cohan, Irving Berlin, and Cole Porter wrote their own lyrics, although Berlin relied on professional harmonizers to write down chord progressions he could only hear. At times, the order of this process was reversed: while Larry Hart always required Richard Rogers's music to get started, Oscar Hammerstein preferred going first, writing lyrics (to a dummy melody's scansion) that Rogers would subsequently orchestrate. In general, however, the standard pattern became the norm, persisting into the rock & roll era. Lieber and Stoller, Goffin and King, and even Jagger and Richards worked in this way, and in doing so, they confirmed the traditional definitions of "the song" and "songwriting."

The metaphysics of this method have become obvious only in retrospect: the division of labor, the priority of music over words, the telos of an AABA song—these aspects of traditional songwriting issue from a culture whose worldview Derrida has labeled "logocentric."[1] Recently, however, new ways of writing songs have begun to challenge the standard procedure. For both *Graceland* and *The Rhythm of the Saints*, Paul Simon built songs up from rhythm tracks—some found, others recorded with no particular song, or even kind of song, in mind. "I waited for the melodies and words to emerge from the tracks," Simon has said about *The Rhythm of the Saints*, but this emergence, unaided by teleology, often had to proceed by trial and error.[2] Having recorded one unaccompanied drum track, Simon worked to "find" a song by trying out genres (New Orleans rhythm & blues, gospel) before settling on doo-wop for what became "The Obvious Child."

Rap composing, of course, is the prototype for this songwriting procedure. Concentrating on rhythm (to the extent of eliminating the vocal melody line), working almost entirely with found music (sampled and recontextualized into new combinations), rap, in one writer's words, "is the scavenger of the music business."[3] In another sense, it represents the pop analogue to a similar activity, one that also turns on knowledge of a tradition that can be reactivated by quotation for new purposes: scholarship. With his 19,000-record collection, Akai S900 sampler, and Ensoniq EPS sequencer (tools for effecting infinite recombinations), Public Enemy's Hank Shocklee seems less like the aural "shoplifter"[4] he has been compared to than the specialist scholar whose impulses, Walter Benjamin observed, lie proximate to those of the collector.[5] As Susan Buck-Morss points out, the collector represented for Benjamin someone "who assembles things that have been set out of circulation and are meaningless as use values,"[6] an apt description of rap composition. Think, for example, of the backing track to De La Soul's "Eye Know," an aural montage of fragments, including the whistling from Otis Redding's "Dock of the Bay" and a horn phrase from Steely Dan's "Peg."

For Benjamin, the scholar and collector resembled still another type that he called "the ponderer," "the man who already had the resolution to great problems, but has forgotten them. . . . The thinking of the ponderer stands therefore in the sign of remembering":

The memory of the ponderer holds sway over the disordered mass of dead knowledge. Human knowledge is piecework to it in a particularly pregnant sense: namely as the heaping up of arbitrarily cut up pieces, out of which one puts together a puzzle. . . . The allegoricist reaches now here, now there, into the chaotic depths that his knowledge places at his disposal, grabs an item out, holds it next to another, and sees whether they fit: that meaning to this image, or this image to that meaning. *The result never lets itself be predicted;* for there is no natural mediation between the two.[7]

The *result never lets itself be predicted*—in this element of surprise lies the great advantage of the ponderer's method. Indeed, the terms of Benjamin's description anticipate communication theory, with its redefinition of information as precisely a function of unpredictability.[8] By this account, then, the initial difficulty of Public Enemy's records issued from the "informational density" of aural collages such as "Fight the Power," with its seventeen different samples in the first ten seconds. This move is not without risks: it increases information by minimizing the redundancy on which easy reception depends. It wins its bet when it tells us something new.

Scholarship, collecting, pondering, information theory—these activities may seem heady company for rap songwriting. Benjamin, however, has taught us to detect the similarities between occupations normally regarded as unrelated, and having done so, we might begin to see in contemporary songwriting suggestions for a new writing practice. What if academics were to write essays the way Paul Simon now composes songs? Given the predictability of so much contemporary criticism, this question seems worth taking up.[9] Hence the form of this essay. I decided to begin with "sampling," building up individual tracks (the essay's rhythm?) by appropriating familiar information, while keeping open the purpose to which it might ultimately be put. I hope that as in rap, while the contents of the individual tracks may sometimes sound familiar, the final mix may be less so.

This essay is composed of six different tracks (two more than the Beatles had at their disposal), conceived at different occasions (as recorded parts might be), and brought together only in the final mix, which you are reading. Just as any modern mixing board allows you to "solo" any given track (to hear it alone, isolated from the others), and just as such soloing is typically the first step in mixing, I will begin here by running down the contents of my individual tracks so that you can see (or hear) the parts before they dissolve into the blend.

Track One. For several years, a group at the University of Florida participated in something called the Institute for European and Comparative Studies (recently renamed the Florida Research Ensemble, to suggest an interest in music and collaborative work), one of many such institutes whose cropping up suggests the increasingly widespread desire for interdisciplinary approaches to subjects perhaps not comprehended by traditional departments—subjects, for example, such as rock & roll. This institute first organized itself around a single topic, the orality/literacy opposition described by Walter Ong, Jack Goody, Jacques Derrida, and others. What interested the group was the notion of writing as a *technology* whose advent and development have dramatically altered human consciousness. As both Ong and Goody demonstrate, a person surrounded by writing thinks differently from someone without it, and he will do so even if he himself cannot write.[10] Abstract definitions, critical analysis, particular logics of ordering—these things that we take for granted in fact depend on the presence of writing and its various apparatuses: lists, indexes, alphabetization, charts, paragraphs. Without writing, the kind of thinking dependent on those categories does not exist.

Here is an example, first described by A. R. Luria and summarized by Ong: given a set of drawings of four objects (a hammer, a saw, a log, and a hatchet), subjects were asked to point to the one dissimilar from the rest. While literate subjects will inevitably exclude log, the one item not a tool, illiterate subjects see the problem differently, not in terms of abstract categories but in terms of practical situations involving use. As Ong observes: "If you are a workman with tools and see a log, you think of applying the tool to it, not of keeping the tool away from what it was made for—in some weird intellectual game." Thus, one peasant replies:

"They're all alike. The saw will saw the log and the hatchet will chop it into small pieces. If one of these has to go, I'd throw out the hatchet. It doesn't do as good a job as a saw." Told that the hammer, saw, and hatchet are all tools, he discounts the categorical class and persists in situational thinking: "Yes, but even if we have tools, we still need wood—otherwise we can't build anything."[11]

Even more important than this example is Ong's conclusion that were he living in a fully alphabetic culture, the peasant would respond differently, would understand the concept of "tool," and would do so even if he himself did not read or write. For my purposes here, I don't intend to develop further the orality/literacy distinction, except to point out the obvious parallel to performance/recording and to suggest that, like writing, recording changes consciousness and that people surrounded by records will develop different attitudes toward music and will do so even if they do not know how to make records themselves.[12]

Track Two. The debates over sampling have called attention to the rapid development in recording technology and the attendant reconceptualization of the recording process. Recording itself has been possible only since 1877, when Edison invented it; writing, of course, is much older, invented by the Sumerians around 3500 B.C. As Ong reminds us, almost everything we take for granted about writing took centuries to arrive: the alphabet itself, for example, appeared two thousand years after the Sumerians' script, and paper was first manufactured in Europe only in the twelfth century. Other familiar uses of writing, Ong points out, arise still later, such as the personal diary, which remained virtually unknown until the seventeenth century.

Recording, by contrast, almost certainly because of writing's existence, has developed more quickly. Nevertheless, most of the major changes have occurred in the last twenty-five years. Before the mid-1960s most engineers and producers, especially those working with jazz and classical artists, regarded their job as capturing a live sound, as simply recording (reproducing) the sound the musicians made while playing together in a room built for its ideal acoustic properties. Again and again, we hear producers such as John Hammond lamenting the difficulties of catching something like the sound of the 1930s Count Basie Band in full flight. In the 1960s Glenn Gould scandalized the classical community by openly acknowledging that his recorded performances consisted of multiple takes joined by inaudible splices. The Beatles made such things famous, with "Strawberry Fields" resulting from two takes, played at different tempos and in different keys, spliced together, and matched by speeding up one and slowing down the other. Simon and Garfunkel's "Bridge over Troubled Water" made the punch-in respectable with the revelation that Garfunkel's vocal had been pieced together from dozens of takes, often of a single word or phrase.

In the 1980s these procedures began to seem primitive. For those musicians still playing in studios (many had been replaced by drum machines and synthesizers), the punch-in (or "drop") became so routine that songs were rarely played all the way through. Recording came more and more to resemble cinematic acting, as mixing (the analogue to editing) *constructed* a performance out of fragments often played on different days (and even in different places: the phenomenon known as "flying in" a part became standard, whereby a musician is sent a multitrack take to which he or she adds his or her part before returning it).[13] And then the explosion of computer-aided recording: MIDI (musical instrument digital interface, the linking together of multiple instruments through a digital signal), sequencing, sampling. The effect of this technology has been increasingly to remove recording from performance, to create sounds that cannot be readily reproduced in live situations. In semiotic terms, a record, like a movie, has become a sign without a referent: behind *Casablanca* or "Fight the Power" lies no single, "real" event that has been transcribed and reproduced. Instead, there are only fragments of behavior, snatches of sound: a turn of the head filmed one Monday for a sequence completed a month later, a drumbeat sampled for mixing with a radio announce-ment. In 1967, situationist leader Guy Debord warned that in "societies where modern conditions of production prevail, all of life presents itself as an im-mense accumulation of *spectacles*. Everything that was directly lived has moved away into a representation."[14] For film and music, we can amend this last sen-tence: "Everything that was directly performed has moved away into a *con-struction*, a recording composed of performance's surviving fragments."

Track Three. It would have been surprising if these developments in recording had *not* begun to affect live performances. If, as Ong points out, the existence of writing modifies the way we speak, we would expect that the existence of recorded music would affect the way people play. And of course it does. From the start, jazz musicians played differently for having heard Louis Armstrong's records.[15]

But I have in mind here less records' influence on musical styles than their impact on protocols of performing, an influence that begins with the rise of the microphone, first for singers (replacing the megaphone, used anachro-nistically by Rudy Vallee), then for orchestral or band sections too quiet to compete with louder instruments. The microphone's redefinition of popular singing, immediately audible in the shift from Jolson's stentorian bravura to Crosby's quiet intimacy, is the first dramatic result of performance's admis-sion of recording technology. This development flourished in rock, first with the spread of the electric guitar and bass, then with sound reinforcement sys-tems (PAs), which by the late 1970s had spawned electronic drums, triggered by hitting the acoustic set. Inevitably, this "contamination" of the live by the recorded has resulted in the actual replacement of the live, as Madonna, Janet Jackson, New Order, Milli Vanilli, and almost every rap group perform to taped music and/or lip-synch to prerecorded vocals. If we want to understand why so many people are upset about this trend, why state legislators in New York and New Jersey have proposed regulating the use of recorded music in live concerts, we need to look at the next track.

Track Four. If Ong's observations about orality and literacy account for record-ing's increasing power to shape performance in its own image, it is Derrida's demonstration of Western culture's historical preference for speech over writ-ing that explains why this process has been so resisted. For, surely, recording amounts to simply another means of writing, and thus it becomes regarded as secondary or supplemental to performance. Indeed, many of the objections raised to the new recording technologies (especially to sampling) reiterate pre-cisely the Platonic objections to writing made in the *Phaedrus*, the dialogue so carefully remarked upon by Derrida.[16] Writing, Plato argued, by providing mankind with an artificial method of storing knowledge, eroded our real powers of memory. Sampling and sequencing, go the current complaints, make musicians unnecessary: you can make records now entirely by recombining bits and pieces sampled from other records; you don't have to play a musical instrument at all.[17]

We can detect here the historical complaint against every new technology and every avant-garde movement that embraces it: the new technology makes things too easy. What previously was possible for only a few (storing large amounts of information, producing a figurative representation of a person or object, making a record) becomes possible for many with, respectively, writing, photography, and sampling. Plato dismissed writing as *artificial* memory. This characterization issued from his own anxious, prescient intuition of all technology's fundamental *automatism,* its potential to continue producing long after the control exacted by human consciousness has been relinquished. For Plato, the ghost in the machine was language that survived not only its author, but also every context of its own enunciation. In the twentieth century that fear has persisted, finding representation in the movies' fatal robots (*Blade Runner*), Frankensteinian monsters devouring assembly lines (*Modern Times*), and computers-run-amok (*2001*). But the rock community has developed an alternative attitude toward its technology's independence. After the Velvet Underground and Jimi Hendrix, concerts frequently ended with guitarists leaving their instruments onstage for the self-sustaining feedback that would accompany the audience's departure. At the other end, the Who began opening shows with "Baba O'Reilly's" programmed synthesizer pattern, set to continue throughout the song. Were these strategies part of a ritual, whose basis was precisely that loss of self that Plato feared? Or were they simply a sanguine (and loud) promise of future songs, future shows?

Disciplines such as film studies and the history of science have shown us that, far from being disinterested, technology follows the route of ideology. Western culture's animus toward writing, therefore, would help to explain why, in a culture of headlong change, recording technology has taken such a relatively long time to develop. If one conceives of live performance as the privileged instance and of recording as only a supplemental means of capturing it, then such things as multitrack tape recorders, reverberation and delay units, compressors, pitch controllers, harmonizers and doublers, and sequencers and samplers will all seem less important, and their invention and implementation will have to wait.

Track Five. I should reveal here something about my own interest in what I am writing about. Since 1982, I have been an active member of a rock band armed with a strange name, for which, I hasten to add, I am not responsible: the Vulgar Boatmen. In fact, as I write, I have just emerged from a two-week session for a second record, during which many of the technologies I have mentioned were used. I will give only one example. For one song, our drummer happened by accident upon an unusual and pleasing snare drum sound. I won't go into details but will mention only that achieving this sound involved a kind of juggling act, holding the drum between the legs so that one foot rested against the lower drum head (slightly muffling the snares) while striking the other head with a combination of cross-sticking and taped brush. Well, it seemed worth it at the time. A week later, however, in mixing, he discovered that for all of its appealing sound, the snare was poorly played (perhaps because it was so difficult to hold), often falling so far behind the beat that any sense of pulse was lost. How to fix it? The drummer started by honoring speech and performance: he wanted to replay the part from start to finish. But five hours' work convinced him that a sound he had achieved by accident could not be reproduced by calculation. He then chose to sample one snare hit (which, after all, he had produced himself) and replay the part by simply triggering this sampled sound in the appropriate, and now properly timed, places.

This process has come to seem normal. What nevertheless still seems strange about the Vulgar Boatmen, especially to the rock press, which never fails to mention this fact when writing about the band, is that there are two sets of Vulgar Boatmen, one in Florida that records and one in Indianapolis that tours. Only one person, the Indianapolis leader, regularly participates in both groups, since he also works on all recordings. While this arrangement derived from practical circumstances (I have a job that prevents my touring, and I have a family; my idea of a tour resembles Brian Eno's: I stay in one place and the audience comes to me), I now realize that having two bands of Vulgar Boatmen enacts the performance/recording dichotomy at the heart of so many debates about contemporary rock & roll. Warhol signaled his acceptance of technology's automatism by calling his studio The Factory, by basing his serial paintings on found photographs, by sending other men to fulfill his speaking engagements. Having cloned ourselves once, the Vulgar Boatmen might become available for franchising—a Vulgar Boatmen in every town, always accompanied by a sign: 6352 records sold.

Track Six. In an issue of the MLA's journal *Profession,* Marianna Torgovnick called for an "experimental critical writing" but admitted that she did not yet know how to produce it.[18] In the past decade, my own courses have asked students to do such experimenting, and I have worked from the assumption, proposed by my colleague Gregory Ulmer, that the avant-garde arts might provide ideal models for different kinds of writing.[19] My own project has been to start with a group of films, the Andy Hardy movies, that beg for the kind of ideological, semiotic, psychoanalytic criticism current in cultural studies but then to prohibit students from taking that conventional approach. Instead, I have asked them to extrapolate from such models as Surrealist games, Derrida's signature experiments (in *Signsponge* and *Glas*), Julian Barnes's *Flaubert's Parrot* (a hybrid text—part novel, part biography, part criticism), Benjamin's *Arcades Project* (a never-finished collage of found material on nineteenth-century Paris), Godard's films and television programs, and Barthes's autobiography (with its alphabetized fragments).[20] Six months ago, when I first thought about this essay, I assumed that recording might provide yet another model for experiments with critical writing, which has traditionally resembled simply transcriptions of spoken lectures. What kind of academic writing, I asked myself, would result from the alphabetic equivalents of such studio effects as reverberation, delay, sampling, flanging, phase-shifting, doubling, equalization, and compression? But just as mixing or editing can often produce a different song or movie from what one expected, so mixing these tracks here has led me to a different conclusion and to three final propositions.

Final Mix. (1) What distinguishes rock & roll from all the music that precedes it—especially classical, Tin Pan Alley, and jazz—is its elevation of the record to primary status. While classical and jazz recordings for the most part aimed only at approximating live performances, regarded as the significant event, many of rock's most important musicians, beginning with Elvis, made records before ever appearing in public. In fact, the performances that began rock & roll, Elvis's Sun recordings, could not be reproduced in any live situation except a very small and empty (to permit reverberation) room, since Elvis's acoustic guitar and Bill Black's acoustic bass simply could not be heard. (Having grown up in Memphis, I know; I attended several early Elvis performances.) Thus, any complaints against Madonna or Janet Jackson for not starting as live performers ignores rock's history.

(2) Derrida and others have alerted us to postmodernism's defining condition: the triumph of an opposition's previously suppressed term. At the end of the twentieth century, we live in a world in which we almost always encounter a representation of something (the Mona Lisa, Mikhail Gorbachev, Bruce Springsteen) before we encounter the thing itself. Where once records hoped only to provide a souvenir of a live performance, concerts now exist to promote records, and to do so they use technology to reproduce as much of the recorded sound, and associated imagery, as possible. In embracing this state of affairs and the technology that has created it, rock affirms its postmodernism. In rejecting this situation, in clinging to speech/performance as the authentic site of musical presence, jazz clings to previous traditions, especially those of modernism.

(3) As I have said, I began preparation for this essay by thinking of record-ing (not songwriting) as a model for academic writing. But I now realize that the relationship is the reverse. For writing, as the more advanced technology, has been the example for recording. What, after all, is sampling except quota-tion, which writers do all the time? What are punch-ins except revisions? What are multitracks but columns? I would argue, however, that *academic* writing, a particularly retrograde subspecialty, continues to make very little use of the technology's resources and that it might begin to notice how much more will-ingly recording engineers, producers, and musicians have begun to experiment with what is possible.

5 How to Start an Avant-Garde

Although its demise is periodically announced—most recently at the hands of that all-purpose assassin-without-passport, "Theory"—the avant-garde survives as an attitude, a temptation, and even an aesthetic practice. Confronted with media culture's voracious powers of assimilation, which can, within a few years, popularize something such as Punk Rock by transforming it first into "New Wave" and later (and more profitably) into "Alternative," the avant-garde seems left without its defining characteristic, its *refusé* status. Indeed, late-twentieth-century Western culture, wired from birth to grave, requires that we reformulate two famous avant-garde maxims: Gertrude Stein's dismissal of Oakland ("There is no there there") and Jean-Luc Godard's definition of film ("Photography is truth, and the cinema is truth twenty-four times a second"). In the land of fax machines, cellular phones, and cable TV, "There is no outside there," and we live under the regime of "Ideology 180,000 times a second."

The avant-garde, of course, has not remained unaffected by this new environment, characterized most of all by *speed*. But to assume that increasingly rapid co-option will destroy the avant-garde ignores how much the avant-garde itself has, throughout its history, promoted its own acceptance. From the start, its preferred analogy was to science, where the route from pure research to applied technology is not only a matter of course, but also a *raison d'être* for the whole enterprise. From this perspective, the avant-gardist's typical complaint about assimilation seems misguided. When the Clash's Joe Strummer denounced fraternity parties' use of "Rock the Casbah" as mindless dance music, he seemed like a chemist protesting the use of his ideas for something as ordinary (and useful) as, let us say, laundry detergent.

The Impressionists, on the other hand, the first avant-garde, understood almost immediately that assimilation was a necessary goal. As a result, those wanting to start a new avant-garde should study their strategies, especially those designed to deal with the one great problem that, since Impressionism, has dictated the shape of the art world—the problem of *the Gap*. As a movement, Impressionism arrived at a moment when art (and, by implication, almost any innovative activity) encountered a new set of circumstances. In particular, for the first time in history, the art world began to assume that between the introduction of a new style and its acceptance by the public, a gap would inevitably exist. As Jerrold Seigel summarizes:

The Impressionists' self-conscious experimentalism, their exploration of the conditions and implications of artistic production in a modern market setting, and their sense that they bore the burden of an unavoidable opposition between innovation in art and society's hostile incomprehension—all made their experience paradigmatic.[1]

There is another, more lyrical, way of putting the matter:

No one is ahead of his time, it is only that the particular variety of creating his time is the one that his contemporaries who are also creating their own time refuse to accept. And they refuse to accept it for a very simple reason and that is that they do not have to accept it for any reason. . . . In the case of the arts it is very definite. Those who are creating the modern composition authentically are naturally only of importance when they are dead because by that time the modern composition having become past is classified and the description of it is classical. That is the reason why the creator of the new composition in the arts is an outlaw until he is a classic, there is hardly a moment in between and it is really too bad very much too bad naturally for the creator but also very much too bad for the enjoyer. . . .

For a very long time everybody refuses and then almost without a pause almost everybody accepts.[2]

Although Gertrude Stein argued that an innovator's contemporaries dismiss his work simply because "they do not have to accept it for any reason," the standard art history account of the matter runs somewhat differently. In the wake of the French Revolution, the decline of the stable patronage system, which had rested on a small sophisticated audience, ready to commission and purchase art, resulted in an entirely new audience for painting—the bourgeoisie, newly come to power (both politically and financially) but less sophisticated, less secure about its own taste. Such an audience (the prototype of the generalist lost in a world of specialization) will inevitably prove conservative, will inevitably lag behind the increasingly rapid stylistic innovations, stimulated in part by this very system (which, after all, is a marketplace, thriving on novelty) and its technology (particularly photography, the technology intervening most directly into painting's realm).

Mass taste, in other words, must be educated to accept what it does not already know. Of course, most mass art (Hollywood, for example) avoids taking on that project and merely reproduces variations of familiar forms. But unless avant-garde artists remain content with posthumous success (represented as the only "genuine" kind by Balzac's *Lost Illusions,* a principal source of the avant-garde's myth), they must work to reduce the gap between the introduction and acceptance of their work. How do they go about doing so? How do you start an avant-garde?

Although the avant-garde carries the reputation of irresponsible rebellion, it, in fact, amounts to the humanities' equivalent of science's pure research. Having derived its name from the military (particularly, from the term for the advance troops entrusted with opening holes in the enemy position) and having repeatedly committed itself to scientifically conceived projects (e.g., Zola's "Experimental Novel," Breton's "Surrealist Manifesto"), the avant-garde has always had its practical side. Indeed, in many ways, it amounts to a laboratory of creativity itself. Thus, the question "How do you start an avant-garde?" has implications for any undertaking where innovation is valuable.

Not surprisingly, sociologists of science have long been interested in this question. More to the point here, a large, although scattered, body of writing has developed around the problem of the gap between the introduction and acceptance of modern art. Tom Wolfe's *Painted Word,* witty and cynical, takes up journalistically what Francis Haskell's "Enemies of Modern Art" and Rosen and Zemer's "Ideology of the Licked Surface: Official Art" treat learnedly.[3] In what follows, although I will refer to those sources, I will draw primarily on what remains the best discussion of the Impressionists' role in the new art world, Harrison and Cynthia White's *Canvases and Careers*.[4] That book makes clear that even if you are a great artist, if you want art to become not a hobby but a paying career, you must attend to the issue of *the Gap*. In fact, you should follow *The Eight Rules for Starting an Avant-Garde*.

1. *Collaboration*. Outsiders working together have a better chance of imposing themselves than does someone working alone. Think of Romanticism (Coleridge and Wordsworth, Goethe and Schiller), Cubism (Picasso and Braque), Surrealism (Breton, Eluard, and Aragon), Deconstruction (Derrida, DeMan, and Miller), Punk Rock (the Sex Pistols, the Clash). Other members of your group will refer to you, cite you, make contacts for you, and collaboration typically proves aesthetically stimulating as well. From the outset, the Impressionists understood this principle. As early as 1864, Monet, Renoir, Sisley, and Bazille painted together in the forest of Fontainebleau, and subsequently they shared Parisian studios or apartments. Even Manet, a relative loner among the Impressionists, maintained an informal salon at the Café Guerbois, where writers (especially Zola) and other artists (e.g., the photographer Nadar) mixed with the painters.

2. *The Importance of the Name*. A crucial factor in the Impressionists' success was the movement's name, which Harrison and Cynthia White point out "was in the great tradition of rebel names. Thrown at them initially as a gibe to provide a convenient handle to insult them, it was adopted by the group in defiance and for want of a better term and made into a winning pennant" (111). "Impressionism" aptly describes much of their work; the name was easy to remember and carried with it the theoretical justification for a style that seemed unfinished, especially when compared to the *fini* or "licked" surface of their official, accepted contemporaries, the *Pompiers*. No avant-garde group has ever achieved major acceptance without a catchy name: think of Futurism, Structuralism, Situationism, the Yale School, Fauvism, *La Nouvelle Vague,* and even Dada, a parody of such names, meaningless, or at least intended to be. The name provides a group identity. Using the "Impressionists," Zola and other critics lumped the individual painters together, and they began to think of themselves as a more coherent group than at first they had actually been. The name provided a hook for critics and dealers, furthering publicity: to review one of the Impressionists was to review them all. The final stage of this group identity generally results in the formation of some official institute or association: the Impressionists formed their own joint stock company, which staged their exhibitions.

3. *The Star*. Avant-garde movements need a key figure whose glamour and prolificness will attract and focus the attention of outsiders. The Impression-

ists had Manet—rich, witty, articulate, and shocking, while also being, by virtue of his training and disposition, the most clearly linked to the great traditions of French painting. Other movements had their own stars:

Cubism:	Picasso
Futurism:	Marinetti
The Bauhaus:	Gropius
Modernism (musical branch):	Stravinsky
Surrealism:	Breton
Relativity:	Einstein
Situationism:	Debord
Abstract Expressionism:	Pollock
Pop Art:	Warhol
La Nouvelle Vague:	Godard
Punk Rock:	Johnny Rotten
Structuralism:	Lévi-Strauss
Semiotics:	Barthes
Deconstruction:	Derrida
Rap:	Public Enemy

4. Traditional Training. Even if you eventually reject its precepts, some encounters with a profession's more or less official schools give you a sense of what to expect. With that work behind you, you have a better chance of justifying your own deviations by demonstrating that you have *chosen* to ignore standards that you have mastered. With the bourgeois audience, nothing helped Picasso's reputation more than his masterful skills in conventional drawing. Almost all of the Impressionists (Cézanne is the great exception) studied at either the École des Beaux-Arts or privately with academic painters. Sometimes the definition of "traditional training" may prove less obvious. With Punk Rock, for example, formal music study mattered far less than extensive experience in working bands: thus, for all its self-propagated myth of amateurism, Punk's important bands always contained pros. Yes, Johnny Rotten and Sid Vicious were novices, but drummer Paul Cook and guitarist Steve Jones were certainly not.

5. The Concept of the Career. The Impressionists demonstrate the effectiveness of refocusing one's attention away from individual paintings, executed for specific occasions designated by a patron, to a whole career and its evolution. Thinking in terms of a career means constructing a narrative that will make sense of an artist's development. *The Gap,* of course, makes such career thinking more subtle, a matter for continual renegotiation. Adopting the extreme long view amounts to accepting a success that will be, at best, posthumous. Stendhal's famous line "I have drawn a lottery ticket whose first prize amounts to this: to be read in 1935" represents the test case. As a publicity gambit, it is perfect, wittily establishing the frame of reference most beneficial to his difficult writing: given wider circulation in his own lifetime, it might even have helped him sell more books. The extent to which Stendhal was content with this ultimate payoff, however, was a direct function of his having other sources of income. An avant-gardist without such independent means should probably adopt Andy Warhol's approach instead: "Business art is the step that comes after Art. I started as a commercial artist, and I want to finish as a business artist."[5]

6. *New Avenues for Distribution and Exhibition.* The Impressionists' *Salons des Refusés,* group shows staged by dealers, and one-man exhibitions are all the equivalent of the new record labels (Punk's Stiff and Rough Trade) and new journals (e.g., *October, Camera Obscura, Diacritics, Substance*) that provide places where off-beat work can appear when the official channels (the major labels, *PMLA*) are closed. Durand-Ruel, the principal Impressionist dealer, founded his own journal. He also opened new markets for art, particularly in America, by redefining art as an investment, a speculation with possibilities of appreciation, thereby enabling sales to that class which understood money more than painting: the bourgeoisie.

7. *Reconceptualization of the Division of Labor.* In the French Academy system, painters (at least those enthroned in the *Institut*) also functioned as judges, selecting the works that appeared in the annual salons. They both painted and set the standards for new painting. Rapidly detecting this conflict of interest, which discouraged the reception of even slightly different work, the Impressionists, perhaps imitating the burgeoning industrial revolution surrounding them, divided the labor: painters stuck to painting, leaving to dealers and critics the task of assessment. In many ways, the avant-garde's history represents a constant tinkering with the division of labor, usually in ways that challenge contemporary arrangements. Thus, with the factory system established as the norm, Duchamp chose to act not only as an artist, but also as his own dealer and critic, thereby recombining the roles the Impressionists had divided. Duchamp's example has become the postmodern standard, with artist/theoretician/publicist figures such as Joseph Beuys, Andy Warhol, Barbara Kruger, and Sherrie Levine.

8. *The Role of Theory and Publicity.* In *The Painted Word,* Tom Wolfe decries Abstract Expressionism's reliance on the criticism that sustained it. That symbiotic relationship, however, began with Impressionism and the period of the new, insecure purchaser. Twentieth-century art made that relationship permanent, requiring, as T. S. Eliot put it, that an innovative artist help create the taste by which his work will be judged. New styles typically demand *a new critical idea.* Impressionism, as many art historians have observed, marked a

shift from arguments about subject matter (deemphasized by many Impressionists) to ones about style. If, according to Wolfe, the key to Abstract Expressionism's success was the concept of *flatness* (which justified nonfigurative painting to a skeptical public), Manet et al. benefited from the concepts of "the impression" and "the painting of modern life," terms that legitimized both the sketchy, unfinished appearance of many Impressionist paintings and their everyday, nonclassical subjects. Even more important, writers favorable to the Impressionists redefined the notion of the artist, who became less an artisan, working for traditional patrons, than a romantic outsider, speculating on future recognition. This new critical idea turned conventional standards upside down. By recasting the Academy as a group of outdated stuffed shirts, vestiges of the *ancien régime*'s hostility toward bourgeois economic and social power, the Impressionists' critics effectively identified the artist with his new client and made rejection by the academy *itself the sign of worth.*

This move proved decisive. The most brilliant discussion of its effects appear in Francis Haskell's "Enemies of Modern Art," which turns on Impressionism's critical reception. Haskell wants to remind us how ugly those paintings once seemed. He quotes Albert Wolff, an important critic, reviewing the second Impressionist exhibition of 1876:

The rue Le Peletier is out of luck. After the burning down of the Opéra, here is a new disaster which has struck the district. An exhibition said to be of painting has just opened at the gallery of Durand-Ruel. The harmless passer-by, attracted by the flags which decorate the façade, goes in and is confronted by a cruel spectacle. Five or six fanatics, one of them a woman, an unfortunate group struck by the mania of ambition, have met there to exhibit their works. Some people split their sides with laughter when they see these things, but I feel heartbroken. These so-called artists call themselves "*intransigeants,*" "Impressionists." They take the canvas, paints and brushes, fling something on at random and hope for the best. (207)

In both its tone and judgment, this passage seems as disastrous as a more famous one that appeared in the *New York Times* in 1956, when television critic Jack Gould reviewed the *Milton Berle Show* appearance of Elvis Presley:

Mr. Presley has no discernible singing ability. His specialty is rhythm songs which he renders in an undistinguished whine; his phrasing, if it can be called that, consists of the stereotyped variations that go with a beginner's aria in a bathtub. For the ear, he is an unutterable bore, not nearly so talented as Frank Sinatra back in the latter's rather hysterical days at the Paramount Theater.[6]

This kind of mistake began with Impressionism, the event that revealed how the gap between the introduction and acceptance of radically new art had become systemic. In "The Ideology of the Licked Surface: Official Art," Rosen and Zemer dramatize this point by concentrating on a single year, 1874, and the painters missing from the Palais du Luxembourg, then France's official museum of modern art: no Manet, no Monet, no Renoir, no Degas, no Cézanne—indeed no painters whom we now consider important: "Over the course of the century," Rosen and Zemer write, "a gap had opened like a trench between the museum and the new art" (218) so that by 1874, the curators had entirely excluded precisely that body of work that future generations would come to regard as the best of its time.

Some of Impressionism's critics were ambivalent about their own responses to these works, whose newness broke with the very forms the writers themselves had previously worked to establish. Indeed, Impressionism prompted its most scrupulous reviewer to articulate, perhaps for the first time, one of the two great dangers facing any critic of any avant-garde: the possibility that one might simply be *too old* to understand what had arrived, the problem that we might call "critical senility." Reviewing the 1868 salon show, Théophile Gautier, one of the best critics of his generation, diagnosed himself:

> Faced with this paradox in painting, one may give the impression—even if one does not admit the charge—of being frightened lest one be dismissed as a philistine, a bourgeois, a Joseph Prudhomme, a cretin with a fancy for miniatures and copies of paintings on porcelain, worse still, as an old fogey who sees some merit in David's *Rape of the Sabines*. One clutches at oneself, so to speak, in terror, one runs one's hand over one's stomach or one's skull, wondering if one has grown pot-bellied or bald, incapable of understanding the audacities of the young. . . . One reminds oneself of the antipathy, the horror aroused some 30 years ago by the paintings of Delacroix, Decamps, Boulanger, Scheffer, Corot, and Rousseau, for so long excluded from the Salon. . . . Those who are honest with themselves, when they consider these disturbing precedents, wonder whether it is ever possible to understand anything in art other than the works of the generation of which one is a contemporary, in other words the generation that came of age when one came of age oneself. . . . It is conceivable that the pictures of Courbet, Manet, Monet, and others of their ilk conceal beauties that elude us, with our old romantic manes already shot with silver threads.[7]

In this new environment, criticism becomes precarious. In 1881 an event occurred that upped the stakes: less than two years before his death, for a rather ordinary effort by his own standards (a painting called *M. Pertuiset, the Lion Hunter*), Manet won the salon's second-place medal. A few months later, thanks to a friend in the Ministry of Arts, he also received the *Légion d'honneur*. The importance of these circumstances, in Francis Haskell's opinion, cannot be overstated:

Manet, the greatest enemy the Academy had ever known, Manet who had been mocked as no other artist ever before him: Manet was now honoured by the Academy, decorated by the State, accepted (however grudgingly) as an artist of major significance. Everything will now be acceptable at the Salons: that is the implication that is drawn from all this. . . . The acknowledgement that there had been a war, but that the critics had (so to speak) lost it and that it was in any case now over, is perhaps the single most important prelude to the development of what we now think of as modern art. (217–218)

From this point on, critics grow wary. Aware of previous mistakes, reviewers become increasingly afraid to condemn anything, since anything might turn out to be the next Manet. Hence, the second of modern criticism's two great dangers, what Max Ernst called *"overcomprehension"* or "the waning of indignation": having propagated the notions of rejection and incomprehensibility as promises of ultimate value, the avant-garde had protected itself from bad reviews.

In initiating this move, Impressionism prefigures postmodernism' s diminished concern for the work of art itself, as opposed to the contexts in which such work might occur. With the rise of what Gerard Genette has called "the paratext," meaning and value become highly negotiable, just like commodities, just like paintings themselves. And theory and publicity turn out to be the principal tools for influencing the ways in which art will acquire meaning.

In the age of Madonna, publicity's importance should be obvious. The Impressionists, however, over a century ago, recognized its role in starting an avant-garde. By the second half of the twentieth century, strange things had become possible. As I discussed in chapter 3, years after his films' release, Douglas Sirk could now completely transform their meaning simply by saying something about them, thereby achieving a Midas-like alchemy that converted forgotten commercial melodramas into celebrated critical "subversions." Since the time when Impressionism first showed us how to start an avant-garde, the role of what has come to be known as Theory has grown enormously. Bohemianism, after all, was from the start what the Goncourt brothers called "a freemasonry of publicity."[8] Indeed, the avant-garde attitude, which since Impressionism has appeared in painting, music, architecture, literature, and film, has begun to enter the realm of criticism itself. The formally experimental work of Roland Barthes and Jacques Derrida offers us the early signs of this move. In retrospect, this development seems inevitable. Given the avant-garde's urgent need to contract *the Gap*, it had to depend on theory as its advocate. Sooner or later, having invented the script for this project, the supporting player would have to take center stage. We have reached that moment now.

6 How to Teach Cultural Studies

1. How to Make a Political Movie

Here is a story. In 1955, when the Indian director Satyajit Ray released *Pather Panchali*, the first part of his *Apu* trilogy, someone asked François Truffaut what he thought of it. Only twenty-three at the time, Truffaut was already a famous, even scandalous, figure on the Paris film scene, notorious for his savage reviews and for his manifesto "A Certain Tendency of the French Cinema," published the year before. That essay had mounted a virulent attack on some of the most important names in the French film industry. "Prevert is to be regretted,"[1] Truffaut had said in that article, thereby denouncing at once the country's most popular poet and the scriptwriter behind such internationally famous movies as *Le Crime de Monsieur Lange*, *Le Jour se Lève*, and *Les Enfants du Paradis*. Of director Jacques Feyder, Truffaut had been even more dismissive: "It really will be necessary," he had announced, "to start an ultimate quarrel with Feyder, before he has dropped definitively into oblivion".[2]

So, Truffaut was asked, what did he think about Ray's movie? And he had an answer: "Why would anyone care about a film about Indian peasants?"

Truffaut, of course, often said such outrageous things—and in writing. Reviewing a British film called *The Quatermass Experiment,* he noted that in one scene, a terrified woman "runs off yelling, but we don't feel sorry for her since she isn't pretty."[3] And in a devastating pan of *Giant,* he observed that although the movie was "everything that is contemptible in the Hollywood system," Elizabeth Taylor at least "is wonderfully beautiful and admirably dressed, which is important."[4]

In today's climate, such remarks appear only in fanzines—and maybe we're the worse for that decorum. For Truffaut's initial response to Ray's movie (he changed his mind after seeing it) states the problem that any political artist faces: Why *should* anyone care about his or her work? Or, to put the matter in the form of a challenge: How do you *make* someone care about Indian peasants?

To try to answer that question, I looked around for some rules about how to make a politically effective film. These are what I found:

Rule #1: "We hate poetry," Keats argued in one of his most famous propositions, "that has a palpable design on us."[5] Even Brecht seemed to agree, insisting in his afterword to *Galileo* on the necessity of "cunning" in presenting the truth. In other words, it won't work to start a film by saying, "We need to remember the plight of Indian peasants," because most people won't care.

Historically, the Right has understood this problem better than the Left. In *Mein Kampf,* Hitler made exactly this point:

It is often a question of overcoming prejudices that are not based on reason, but, for the most part unconsciously, are supported only by sentiment. To overcome this barrier of instinctive aversion, of emotional hatred, of prejudiced rejection, is a thousand times harder than to correct a faulty or erroneous scientific opinion. False concepts and poor knowledge can be eliminated by instruction, the resistance of the emotions never. Here only an appeal to those mysterious powers themselves can be effective.[6]

In summary, work by indirection. The head-on confrontation won't do.

Rule #2: In April 1934, just fifteen months after Hitler had come to power, Walter Benjamin insisted "that the tendency of a literary work can only be politically correct if it is also literately correct."[7] For Brecht, "literary correctness," at least in a popular form such as the commercial theater, ultimately came to mean pleasure. "From the first," he wrote in his 1949 manifesto, "A Short Organum for the Theatre," "it has been the theatre's business to entertain people, as it also has all of the other arts. It is this business which always gives it its particular dignity; it needs no other passport than fun, but this it has got to have."[8]

Thus, work on your art at least as much as on your political position. Remember your audience.

Rule #3: When the painter Degas complained that he didn't understand why he couldn't write better sonnets since he had so many "ideas," Mallarmé famously replied, "But my dear Degas, you don't make sonnets with ideas, but with *words.*"[9] Or as Sartre once put it, "One isn't a writer for having chosen to say certain things, but for having chosen to say them in a certain way."[10]

These propositions imply that art results from hundreds of decisions about technical problems: the painter worries about the design of a hat in the upper-left-hand corner, the writer about the choice of a word, the musician about a drum sound in the second chorus. From this perspective, Truffaut's outrageous propositions begin to make practical sense as a challenge to the high-minded, politically correct, but deadly films he was attacking: if an actor isn't physically attractive, the audience will have a harder time sympathizing with her character.

A film is not made from ideas but from images and sounds. Thus, in the cinema, appearances become enormously important.

2. How to Start an Avant-Garde

With its emphasis on aesthetics and discrediting of politics, Truffaut's writings proved vital to what became the most important movement in film history—the French New Wave. Because the New Wave directors—especially Truffaut, Jean-Luc Godard, Eric Rohmer, and Jacques Rivette—all began as film critics for André Bazin's *Cahiers du Cinéma, La Nouvelle Vague* not only spawned an entirely new style of filmmaking, it also invented film studies. The *Cahiers'* championing of directors (announced as *la politique des auteurs*), its detailed interviews with favored filmmakers (e.g., Rossellini and Hitchcock), and its attention to out-of-the way movies all stimulated interest in the cinema and its history. Indeed, the agenda established by *auteurism* dominated the first decades of academic film study, with courses devoted to precisely the directors canonized by Truffaut et al. (Hitchcock, Bergman, Rossellini, Hawks, Ford, and Welles) and to their favored genres (particularly the Western).

In retrospect, its international success made the New Wave seem inevitable. The facts, however, remain startling. When "A Certain Tendency of the French Cinema" appeared in the January 1954 issue of the *Cahiers du Cinéma,* Truffaut was only twenty-one years old. That polemic, disguised as an essay, called for an overthrow of the French film establishment while suggesting that the country wasn't big enough to hold both a hack like Claude Autant-Lara and a master like Jean Renoir. Truffaut could not have been clearer: "I do not believe," he wrote, "in the peaceful co-existence of the 'Tradition of Quality' and an '*auteur*'s cinema'" (234). In 1954, Truffaut was unknown outside of the *Cahiers* circle. Five years later, the New Wave had won, using the success of *The 400 Blows* (Truffaut), *Hiroshima Mon Amour* (Resnais), and *Breathless* (Godard) to sweep away the "certain tendency of the French cinema" that Truffaut had denounced.

This remarkable success, an instant avant-garde, had begun, quite literally, as a pedagogical project. In the years after World War II, André Bazin had embarked on his adventures in what Americans call "continuing education." As the Director of Cultural Services for *L'Institut des Hautes Études Cinématographiques* (*IDHEC*) and subsequently as the director of a "center for cinematographic initiation" within the leftist organization *Travail et Culture,* Bazin visited factories, union halls, and schools, giving lectures, scheduling films and speakers, and writing program notes and reviews. In April 1951, after this period of "organization and animation," the first issue of the *Cahiers du Cinéma,* co-founded by Bazin, appeared. Then, during a twelve-month period in 1952 and 1953, Bazin published "The Evolution of the Language of Cinema" and "The Virtues and Limitations of Montage," essays attacking the two most prestigious schools of filmmaking, Soviet montage and German Expressionism, and proposing a more radical possibility for the cinema. The Soviets and the Germans, according to Bazin, had betrayed the cinema's sacred purpose, "the recreation of the world in its own image," by "putting their faith in the image" instead of in reality, convulsing the camera's objectivity with abstracting montages and grotesque *mise-en-scènes.*[11]

With Bazin as editor in chief, the *Cahiers* critics began to formulate a position that shifted attention from Bazin's automatic camera to *la politique des auteurs*' great filmmakers. Redefined as heroic individualists, struggling against the constraints of Hollywood's studio system, the *Cahiers*' favored directors were represented as having imposed their own wills in even the most collaborative situations. From 1954 to 1960, the *Cahiers* group refined this position into a platform that simultaneously encouraged their own eventual filmmaking and made sense of it. In doing so, they were teaching themselves and their future audiences how to invent an experimental movement.

The French New Wave, like every avant-garde, worked by extrapolation. In *Heuretics: The Logic of Invention,* Gregory Ulmer demonstrates that creativity works more systematically than popular mythology assumes, proceeding as much by emulation as inspiration. In fact, Ulmer argues, avant-garde manifestos "belong to the tradition of the discourse on method" and "tend to include a common set of elements." Those elements, he suggests, can be mnemonically summarized by the acronym CATTt, representing the following operations:

C = Contrast
A = Analogy
T = Theory
T = Target
t = tale (or form in which the avant-garde will work)[12]

Look, for example, at perhaps the century's most famous avant-garde statement of intent, "The Surrealist Manifesto."[13] Breton's opening move involved *Contrast,* his opposition to literary realism and its conceptual bases, traditional reason and logic. For an *Analogy,* Breton, recalling his medical training, proposed that Surrealism take up the scientific model of experimentation and research. For *Theory,* Breton borrowed Freudian psychoanalysis, aiming at an immediate *Target* of the arts, but ultimately at everyday life itself. Surrealism's *tale* would become the traditional arts and *ad hoc* provocations, both conceived of as conceptual interventions into politics and what Trollope once called "the way we live now."

Since avant-gardes develop by using models found in other disciplines, this method depends on translation. Surrealism, for example, an aesthetic/political movement, derived from Freudian psychoanalysis, but Freud found his offspring unrecognizable. That response suggests how high-handed and free the translation process can become. Indeed, in a very real sense, the method resembles that aspect of photography objected to by Susan Sontag, the "taking" that honors no original context:

To photograph is to appropriate the thing photographed. . . . In a world ruled by photographic images, all borders ("framing") seem arbitrary. Anything can be separated, made discontinuous from anything else: all that is necessary is to frame the subject differently.[14]

Brecht, on the other hand, proposed a more sanguine metaphor for this borrowing-for-other-purposes, the *Messingkauf,* the purchaser of brass:

I can only compare myself with a man, say, who deals in scrap metal and goes up to a brass band to buy, not a trumpet, let's say, but simply brass. The trumpeter's trumpet is made of brass, but he'll hardly want to sell it as such, by its value as brass, as so many ounces of brass. All the same, that's how I ransack your theater for events between people, such as you do more or less imitate even if your imitations are for a very different purpose than my satisfaction. To put it in a nutshell: I'm looking for a way of getting incidents between people imitated for certain purposes; I've heard that you supply such imitations; and now I hope to find out if they are actually the kind of imitations I can use.[15]

Avant-gardists and the French New Wave directors were no exception, always in the position of the *Messingkauf,* looking for something they can use.

If we take as the New Wave's manifesto three essays, Alexandre Astruc's *"La Caméra Stylo,"*[16] Truffaut's "A Certain Tendency of the French Cinema," and Godard's 1962 interview with the *Cahiers du Cinéma,*[17] we can observe the same pattern of invention.

Contrast: "The tradition of quality," those formally conservative, big-budget French films controlled by scriptwriters rather than directors. By suggesting that this tradition combined middlebrow subject matter with "scholarly framing, complicated lighting effects, 'polished' photography," Truffaut linked that tradition to the nineteenth-century salon painting against which Impressionism had revolted.[18] In 1958, *Cahiers* critic Louis Marcorelles made that connection explicit, observing that the establishment French cinema, "missing the turning towards neo-realism which it might have taken, moved instead towards academicism and the great 'machine' constructions of directors such as Clément and Clouzot."[19] Opposing this new version of what art historians have called "the licked surface,"[20] the New Wave celebrated the rough look of Italian neorealism and American B-movies.

Analogy: Astruc, Truffaut, and Godard all rely on the literary notion of authorship and writing: the camera will become a *stylo* when filmmakers become like writers. Godard insisted on this link:

I think of myself as an essayist, producing essays in novel form or novels in essay form: only instead of writing, I film them. Were the cinema to disappear, I would simply accept the inevitable and turn to television; were television to disappear, I would revert to pencil and paper. For there is a clear continuity between all forms of expression. It's all one.[21]

Theory: The traditionally romantic notions of self-expressive (and proprietary) authorship, but even more immediately, Sartre's existentialist insistence on individual responsibility. After all, the issue of who was to be responsible for what appeared on the screen remained the question that defined New Wave practice. The Target, of course, was the French film industry, and the tale, or form, that hybrid of documentary and fiction that Godard labeled "research in the form of a spectacle."[22]

Just as this method of invention-by-appropriation thrives on infidelity to the theoretical source (Breton did not want to be a doctor), it can also work with something less than a profound knowledge of it (Breton had not read all of Freud). The avant-gardist is always in the position of the photographer who can extract a beautiful image from something he knows little about. We will probably never learn exactly how much of Sartre Astruc, Truffaut, and Godard had read. We do know that by the time the *Cahiers* proclaimed *La Politique des Auteurs,* Sartre and his vocabulary had entered what Sherry Turkle calls "a sociology of superficial knowledge."[23] His 1945 lecture "Existentialism Is a Humanism," printed in a cheap paperback version in 1946, had become the breviary of that movement, and the echoes of his phrasing are unmistakable in Godard:

Man is nothing else but that which he makes of himself . . . man is responsible for what he is. Thus, the first effect of existentialism is that it puts every man in possession of himself as he is, and places the entire responsibility for his existence squarely upon his own shoulders. (Sartre)[24]

The cinema is not a craft. It is an art. It does not mean teamwork. One is always alone: on the set as before the blank page. (Godard)[25]

[T]he moral choice is comparable to the construction of a work of art. (Sartre)[26]

A dolly shot is a moral statement. (Godard)[27]

Who can give an answer to that [a moral dilemma] *à priori?* No one. . . . You are free, therefore choose—that is to say, invent. No rule of general morality can show you what you ought to do: no signs are vouchsafed in this world. (Sartre)[28]

The problem which has long preoccupied me . . . is: why do one shot rather than another? . . . What is it ultimately that makes one run a shot on or change to another? A director like Delbert Mann probably doesn't think this way. He follows a pattern. Shot—the character speaks; reverse angle, someone answers. (Godard)[29]

This is what I thought: for the most banal event to become an adventure, you must (and this is enough) begin to recount it. (Sartre)[30]

People pigeon-hole adventure. "We're off on holiday," they say, "the adventure will begin as soon as we are at the seaside." They don't think of themselves as living the adventure when they buy their train tickets, whereas in the film everything is on the same level: buying train tickets is as exciting as swimming in the sea. (Godard)[31]

While these parallels suggest why the French New Wave directors insisted on the notion of authorship (in fact a code term for the more metaphysical, and *au courant,* idea of *responsibility*), they do not tell us why these men also championed the image. That secret lies in the movement's buried connections to another theory, Surrealism. Almost certainly, the *Cahiers* critics knew that earlier avant-garde less from its works than from the extraordinary, Surrealist-inspired screening practices of Henri Langlois's *Cinémathèque Française*. In a theater where foreign-language films ran without subtitles, where programs changed without notice, where movies collided unpredictably without regard for genre, period, or assumed value, the New Wave directors, "the children of the *Cinémathèque*," experienced "the heightened, autonomous image"[32] that Breton and his colleagues had sought through their own eccentric moviegoing:

> When I was "at the cinema age" . . . I never began by consulting the amusement pages to find out what film might chance to be the best, nor did I find out what time the film was to begin. I agreed wholeheartedly with Jacques Vaché in appreciating nothing so much as dropping into a cinema when whatever was playing was playing, at any point in the show, and leaving at the first hint of boredom—of surfeit—to rush off to another cinema where we behaved in the same way, and so on. . . . I have never known anything more *magnetising:* it goes without saying that more often than not we left our seats without even knowing the title of the film, which was in no way of importance to us. On a Sunday several hours sufficed to exhaust all that Nantes could offer us: the important thing is that one came out "charged" for a few days.[33]

The New Wave, in other words, invented itself by combining Existentialism and Surrealism, movements whose lessons and strategies it translated into another domain—filmmaking. There, "responsibility" reappeared as "authorship," and the decontextualized image as *"mise-en-scène,"* forced to live side by side as incompatible intellectual heirs. When we remember that another figure who acknowledged similar intellectual debts, Roland Barthes, listed "fidelity" as one of his "Dislikes,"[34] and when we consider that Truffaut, who had sympathized with translation, ended up, in Godard's eyes, making the kind of films he had earlier denounced, we might consider this maxim: the more unfaithful the translator, the more original the work of art.

3. How to Teach Cultural Studies

Fourteen years after "A Certain Tendency of the French Cinema," a political crisis threatened New Wave filmmaking and the *Cahiers* writers who supported it. In the wake of May 1968, everything changed in film culture, and Truffaut's brand of aestheticism seemed suddenly suspect. The *Cahiers du Cinéma* now faced a problem; its editors and writers wanted to take up politics, but looking around for films to champion, they discovered that most of the politically correct movies were bad.

They shouldn't have been surprised. Truffaut, after all, had been reacting against an earlier wave of politically correct cinema, both in France and the United States, and he had detected the problem: the filmmakers had assumed that their ideas, not their images, were the important thing. Since most of the French examples Truffaut cited are unknown to us (a sign of their fall from film history), the American examples might help. Known as "problem pictures" (often produced by *auteurist bête noir* Stanley Kramer), these movies earnestly portrayed cruelties caused by racial prejudice (*Gentleman's Agreement, Pinky, Home of the Brave, The Defiant Ones, Intruder in the Dust*), the sufferings of maltreated mental patients (*The Snake Pit*), alcohol or drug addiction (*Come Back, Little Sheba; The Man with the Golden Arm; The Lost Weekend*). For the most part, time has confirmed the *Cahiers* position that they were also very dull movies.

The scandal of early *auteur* criticism had been to replace this canon (the critically acclaimed and Academy Award–winning one) with an alternative list of B-movies (such as *Gun Crazy* and *The Narrow Margin*) and films made by action directors such as Raoul Walsh, Howard Hawks, and Nicholas Ray. What the *Cahiers* had admired about these movies was their specifically cinematic qualities. In a 1957 article, "Nothing but Cinema," Godard had observed of *Rebel without a Cause* that "one cannot but feel that here is something which exists only in the cinema, which would be nothing in a novel, the stage, or anywhere else, but which becomes fantastically beautiful on the screen."[35]

After May 1968, this position seemed less valid. Brecht, in fact, had been nervous about it long before. Walter Benjamin reported that in 1934, Brecht had admitted that he often imagined being interrogated by a tribunal. " 'Now tell us, Mr. Brecht, are you really in earnest?' 'I would have to admit that no, I'm not completely in earnest. I think too much about artistic problems, you know, about what is good for the theater, to be completely in earnest.' "[36]But what could the *Cahiers* critics do without some decent, politically satisfactory films to write about? Here is what they did do: they invented a way of looking at the movies that suggested that as a measure of political correctness, a film's *form* was even more important than its content. From this perspective, a film such as Godard's *Breathless*, with its nonpolitical subject matter but its iconoclastic form, became more "subversive" than something such as *Norma Rae*, radical thematically but absolutely straightforward formally.

But even better, in developing their taxonomy of films and their relationship to what the *Cahiers* had begun calling "dominant ideology," the *auteur* group invented the now-famous *category e:*

Films which seem at first sight to belong firmly within the ideology and to be completely under its sway, but which turn out to be so only in an ambiguous manner. An internal criticism is taking place which cracks the film apart at its seams . . . thus, many Hollywood films end up by partially dismantling the system from within.[37]

Not surprisingly, *category e* promptly filled up with all the old *auteurist* favorites: John Ford, Howard Hawks, Hitchcock, Nicholas Ray.

I don't mean to sound cynical about this move. In fact, I owe my whole career to *category e,* since I based the book that earned me tenure entirely on this hermeneutic *coup.* But the need to develop *category e* attests to the persistent appeal of movies that are aesthetically interesting.

Godard, however, was impatient with this interpretive feat. Renouncing his earlier work as "bourgeois," he began producing a series of explicitly political works now signed by "The Dziga Vertov Group": *Wind from the East, British Sounds, Struggle in Italy.* These films, even for Godard aficionados, now seem unwatchable. Nevertheless, they provide a lesson. In his earlier films, Godard had achieved a political effect by indirection, out of the accumulation of details resulting from the hundreds of technical choices concerning the contents of individual shots and their articulation. To take just one example, think of the famous moment in *Vivre sa Vie,* when Nana, evicted from her apartment, desperate, sits composing a job application letter to a madam. Trying to describe herself, and to provide her exact measurements, she stands up and silently, quickly measures herself with her thumb and forefinger. That gesture, by suggesting the link between Nana's childlike naïveté and her victimization, seems profoundly political. But it also remains visually memorable in a way that so little of Godard's Dziga Vertov–period films do.

Years earlier, Truffaut had repeatedly singled out such moments as the key to filmmaking. An ordinary Melville movie could be redeemed by shots of "Pigalle at daybreak," Vadim's *And God Created Woman* by an incidental moment of Brigitte Bardot lifting in her arms a little girl trying to grab a newspaper placed just out of her reach.[38]

Thus, we return to the basic rule for making successful political art: think about the art first. The best example of a contemporary artist who has operated in this way, whose work has had enormous political impact, and who has become perhaps the most important artist of the past twenty years is Cindy Sherman. In her interviews, she admits to being "shy of theory, intellectually reticent." Responding to the flood of deconstructive, psychoanalytic, Marxist, and feminist readings of her work, she has said: "I like to read these kinds of analyses because they have nothing at all to do with anything that made me produce the works concerned. Still, the fact that they exist is very interesting. They're a kind of side effect."[39]

If this position seems reactionary or ostrich-like, maybe we should remember how hard it is to be good at everything: politics, art, interpretation, promotion, etc. When Godard was at his best, he seemed to think most about technical problems (where and when to begin a shot, where and how to end it). But in *2 or 3 Things I Know about Her,* a movie that took the aesthetics-politics marriage as an explicit subject, he ended the famous garage sequence, in which his voice-over constantly questioned the choices that had produced what appeared on screen ("Am I looking from too close or from too far away?"), with this confession: "I am only looking for reasons to be happy. Should I have talked about Juliette or the leaves? Since in any case it was impossible to have done both, let us just say that both were trembling gently at the beginning of the end of that October afternoon."

Let us imagine that teaching cultural studies has something to do with both political filmmaking and starting an avant-garde. In the last two decades, English as a discipline has attempted to assimilate the ideological critique that arose in film studies after May 1968. The name for that assimilation is cultural studies. Its first moves now seem familiar: the creation of a new canon and the use of *category e* ingenuity to salvage the traditional one. But this avant-garde, having redefined aesthetics as an ideological category, has revived the political correctness dismissed by Truffaut. If May 1968 made us aware of the political blindness behind, for example, Truffaut's remark that "we don't feel sorry for her since she isn't pretty," *la Politique des Auteurs* had taught us the limitations of politics divorced from aesthetics.

Cultural studies now faces its first significant backlash, symptomized by John Ellis's *Literature Lost: Social Agendas and the Corruption of the Humanities* and by the recently announced abdications from "Theory" of Frank Lentricchia ("Last Will and Testament of an Ex-Literary Critic") and Jane Tompkins ("Me and My Shadow," *A Life in School*).[40] But surely the answer lies not in simply a "Return to Literature" that would repudiate what cultural studies has taught us. At the end of every class, these days, teachers find themselves in Godard's position, torn between talking about aesthetics or politics. This impasse, now two centuries old, seems at times to offer no escape. In fact, the way out depends on invention. In this new educational era marked by vocationalism, decreased funding, and contracting job markets, the humanities' traditional ways of doing business cannot survive. If Gregory Ulmer is right, their replacement will require the kind of extrapolation typical of all avant-gardes and of the New Wave in particular. Some of the slots have started to fill:

Contrast: conventional academic writing and pedagogy, formally conservative and devoted to critique.

Analogy: the avant-garde arts as the research dimension of the humanities, the equivalent of pure science.

Theory: ?

Target: university education.
tale: ?

The cultural studies project has become clear: we must experiment with different ways of completing this *CATTt*. The future of pedagogy in an age of electronic reproduction depends on our doing so.

7 The Mystery of Edward Hopper

Anyone writing about Edward Hopper's relationship to the cinema faces an obvious difficulty: while the evidence of Hopper's interest in the movies is certain, the facts about what he actually saw and liked are few—a stray remark, for example, praising an obscure American film, *The Savage Eye;* a line stating his eagerness to see Jean-Luc Godard's *Breathless.*[1] Working from the paintings themselves, one can, of course, infer certain connections: the diners in Hemingway's "The Killers" and Warner Brothers' *Little Caesar* become *Nighthawks,* which itself appears, as an explicit citation, in the film *Pennies from Heaven.* Similarly, Hopper's eerie chiaroscuro, abandoned urban settings, and odd perspectives (often of an anonymous passerby) all appear in the thirties crime movies that evolved into film noir. While this approach might prove interesting, it would ultimately depend on intuitive speculation and biographical research. This essay takes a different path.

In one of art history's founding myths, photography freed painting to become nonfigurative: hence the century-long rush from Impressionism to Abstract Expressionism, with its stops along the way at the stations whose names now evoke memories of realism's apparently unchecked dissolution—Fauvism, Cubism, Futurism, Dada. In this explanatory system, Edward Hopper, always an idiosyncratic artist, starts to seem even more strange. When Hopper was born, photography, after all, was over fifty years old, Joseph Nicéphore Niepce having managed in 1827 to take the first photograph, a view of his own courtyard, from an upper window of his chateau. And yet, after an early brush with a very belated Impressionism, Hopper remained that puzzling anomaly of pre-Pop twentieth-century art: an important figurative painter.

Transforming art history into a different kind of story, we could imagine this case as *The Mystery of Edward Hopper,* a tale that would concern not so much a murder as an apparent *disappearance*—the vanishing of photography and its presumably dispositive influence on painting. For if art history's account is true, how could Hopper, a resident of one of the world's great centers of photography, have escaped that medium's supposedly irresistible prompting to paint in a *different way?* This question suggests an alternate route of investigation only beginning to be explored: the profound impact of photography on painting, and indeed on cognition as a whole, may not be limited to the abandonment of realism. It may involve *something else.* Locating that *something else* will require me to follow specific clues.

First clue: Almost one hundred and seventy years after its invention, photography has finally become recognized as the first development in a communications revolution whose later stages—the cinema, videotape, and the computer—have made visible photography's decisive break with alphabetic culture. In *Orality and Literacy,* Walter Ong has summarized the implications of such a break, describing the research tradition (named "grammatology" by philosopher Jacques Derrida) that posits that different technologies of communication occasion different ways of thinking.[2] An oral culture, for example, relying entirely on human memory to store and retrieve its information, develops particular conceptual habits that appear strange to us, the inhabitants of a fully alphabetic society.[3] Grammatology further suggests that history has seen only two major revolutions in communications technology: the first involved precisely this shift from oral to alphabetic cultures; the second, the transition from alphabetic to "electronic," we are living through now. In fact, the much-debated word "postmodernism" is best understood as simply the term for that moment when awareness of this second transition becomes widespread. What are the consequences, characteristics, and modes of an age of film, television, magnetic tape, and computers? How will what we call "thinking" change with this technology? In fact, Hopper's paintings suggest answers to these questions.

Second clue: One of the first writers to point to photography's grammatological significance was Walter Benjamin. In his most famous essay, "The Work of Art in the Age of Mechanical Reproduction" (1935), Benjamin designated photography as the crucial first step toward something other than alphabetic literacy.[4] Photography, he argued, changed everything, forcing us to rethink art and writing and even thinking itself. At places in another essay, "A Small History of Photography," Benjamin seemed merely to be contributing to the art-history party line about the relationship between photography and painting: the calling-card daguerreotype, Benjamin observed, had quickly put nineteenth-century portrait painters out of business.[5] But elsewhere he insisted on photography's more radical consequences, and he was willing to act on his argument. *The Arcades Project,* his proposed study of nineteenth-century Paris, remains the great unbuilt prototype of a new, explicitly "electronic" history, relying less on traditional exposition than on the forms basic to photography and film: collage and montage. And in aphoristic notes, Benjamin left hints about the *Arcades Project*'s intended focus:

To someone looking through piles of old letters, a stamp that has long been out of circulation on a torn envelope often says more than a reading of dozens of pages.[6]

The eternal would be the ruffles on a dress rather than an idea.[7]

Third clue: Benjamin had derived his idea for the *Arcades Project* from Louis Aragon's 1926 Surrealist narrative *Le Paysan de Paris.*[8] "At night in bed," Benjamin later wrote, "I could never read more than two or three pages at a time, for my heartbeat became so strong that I was forced to lay the book down."[9] The encounter with Aragon's book clinched Benjamin's interest in Surrealism. Its preoccupation with dislocation, its attention to fragments, and its concentration on *le quotidien* all ensured that Surrealism as a movement would be drawn to photography. Its founder, André Breton, defined his invention of automatic writing as "the true photography of thought," and, as Rosalind Krauss has pointed out, all three of Surrealism's examples of beauty (mimicry, "the expiration of movement," and the found object) were explicitly photographic.[10]

The Surrealists, however, did not stop with photography. They quickly embraced its implementation in the cinema, anticipating Jean-Luc Godard's dictum that "photography is the truth, and the cinema is the truth twenty-four times a second."[11] Above all, the movies offered Breton and his colleagues examples of the event they most valued: the eruption of "the marvelous" into everyday life. In Aragon's words:

All our emotion exists for those dear old American adventure films that speak of daily life and manage to raise to a dramatic level a banknote on which our

attention is riveted, a table with a revolver on it, a bottle that on occasion becomes a weapon, a handkerchief that reveals a crime. . . . [12]

For the Surrealists, the ability to notice such things depended upon tactics of fragmentation, which they redefined as a means to knowledge. Thus, such maneuvers as Breton's moviegoing habits (which depended on ignorance of both the films' titles and their showing times) and Man Ray's trick of isolating details by watching the screen through barely parted fingers were intended to release individual images from the narratives that constrained them. Under normal conditions, for example, you would never notice a wrinkled map, spread casually across a writing table, when the story was telling you to look at the gun in the heroine's pocket. But, the Surrealists had asked, what if the *map* contained the potential for revelation, and the movie made you miss it? Or, as Benjamin speculated, "What form do you suppose a life would take that was determined at a decisive moment precisely by the street song last on everyone's lips?"[13]

The movies, the Surrealists recognized, had revealed "photographic think-ing's" reliance on the relationship between sequence and fragment. For train-ing in how to notice something like Benjamin's out-of-circulation stamp, the cinema became a crucial site, for with the movies' power both to illuminate everyday details and to make them disappear, film was at once the miracle cure and the old problem. On one hand, by extracting its people and objects from the world at large, the cinema made them more visible than ever before. Aragon described the mechanism and its effect:

To endow with a poetic value that which does not yet possess it, to willfully re-strict the field of vision so as to intensify expression: these are two properties that help make cinematic décor the adequate setting of modern beauty.[14]

On the other hand, by subjecting every detail to what Noël Burch has called "linearization"—in other words, by making every aspect of the image subser-vient to the narrative—the movies radically discouraged the kind of attention that notices a forgotten stamp instead of an obvious letter.[15]

For the Surrealists, the solution involved tactics of dislocation that would pry images loose from the stories constraining them. Hence the strange ur-gency of Breton's description of his early moviegoing:

When I was "at the cinema age" . . . I never began by consulting the amusement pages to find out what film might chance to be the best, nor did I find out the time the film was to begin. I agreed wholeheartedly with Jacques Vaché in ap-preciating nothing so much as dropping into the cinema when whatever was playing was playing, at any point in the show, and leaving at the first hint of boredom—of surfeit—to rush off to another cinema where we behaved in the same way. . . . I have never known anything more *magnetising*: it goes without saying that more often than not we left our seats without even knowing the title of the film, which was of no importance to us anyway. On a Sunday several hours sufficed to exhaust all that Nantes could offer us: the important thing is that one came out "charged" for a few days. . . . [16]

This description corresponds in important ways to the experience of seeing a series of Hopper's paintings, many of which encourage us to imagine the larger narrative from which a single incident might have been drawn. What will happen next to the woman barely glimpsed through *Night Windows?* What stranger will appear as night falls and the lights come on at the lonely filling station, somewhere in the countryside, in *Gas?* The preoccupation with the fragment and, in particular, with the capacity of the film still (real or imaginary) to enter into or evoke different sequences provides the *raison d'être* of such works as Joseph Cornell's Surrealist movie *Rose Hobart* (derived from the pulp melodrama *East of Borneo*), Cindy Sherman's *Film Stills*, and a collage film such as Chick Strand's *Loose Ends.*

For Breton and his colleagues, the tactic of fragmentation applied to the cinema merely imitated the moments when everyday structures collapse and ordinary details, entering into unusual juxtapositions, take on, if only temporarily, attributes of "the marvelous." Moving, coincidences, getting lost, or even love could provoke the desired vision. As Benjamin described the sensation,

Breton and Nadja are the lovers who convert everything that we have experienced on mournful railway journeys (railways are beginning to age), on godforsaken Sunday afternoons in the proletarian quarters of the great cities, in the first glance through the rain-blurred window of a new apartment, into revolutionary experience, if not action. They bring the immense forces of "atmosphere" concealed in these things to the point of explosion.[17]

The extent to which Hopper shared this sensibility shows itself in a remarkably similar passage he wrote in praise of fellow artist Charles Burchfield:

From what is to the mediocre artist and unseeing layman the boredom of everyday existence in a provincial community, he has extracted that quality we may call poetic, romantic, lyric, or what you will. By sympathy with the particular he has made it epic and universal. No mood has been so mean as to seem unworthy of interpretation; the look of an asphalt road as it lies in the broiling sun at noon, cars and locomotives lying in God-forsaken railway yards, the streaming summer rain that can fill us with such hopeless boredom, the blank concrete walls and steel constructions of modern industry, mid-summer streets with the acid green of close-cut lawns, the dusty Fords and gilded movies—all the sweltering, tawdry life of the American small town, and behind all, the sad desolation of our suburban landscape. He derives daily stimulus from these, that others flee from or pass with indifference.[18]

Fourth clue: Of the writers who created what we have come to call "contemporary theory" (otherwise known as "cultural studies"), Roland Barthes is the most obvious heir to the Surrealist concern with the sequence-fragment opposition. Admitting his own "resistance to the cinema," Barthes proposed that if the movies' relentless unrolling prevents your noticing anything except narratively underlined details, the only response is to stop the film.[19] In his essay "The Third Meaning," Barthes did just that, working not with Eisenstein's films but with individual frames taken from them. In suppressing the movies' continuity, he had, in effect, managed to simulate the experience of traveling in a foreign country without knowing the language. More exactly, he was reinventing Breton's experiment of entering an unidentified film *in medias res* and leaving when its point became too clear.[20]

Perusing images liberated from their plots, Barthes discovered his attention drawn to details (a woman's scarf, an eyebrow's curve) whose significance he could attribute to neither information nor symbolism. This "third meaning" (or "obtuse meaning"), Barthes wrote, "is a signifier without a signified," "is outside (articulated) language," "is discontinuous, indifferent to the story and to the obvious meaning." Indeed, "it outplays meaning—subverts not the content but the whole practice of meaning."[21]

What Barthes had located was the point where, to use Walter Ong's formulation, alphabetic culture gives way to the photographic. Barthes made that proposition explicit:

It is at the level of the third meaning, and at that level alone, that the "filmic" finally emerges. The filmic is that in the film which cannot be described, the representation which cannot be represented. The filmic begins only where language and metalanguage end. Everything that can be said about *Ivan* [*the Terrible*] or *Potemkin* can be said of a written text . . . except this, the obtuse meaning.[22]

Barthes's insight involved recognizing these "third meanings" as a means to a knowledge whose starting point was the "interrogative reading" they compelled. In effect, Barthes was converting *fetishism,* with its overvaluation of apparently trivial details, into a research strategy, one that would enable its practitioner to enter a problem at other than the designated points.[23] The representation of this strategy appears in two movies where photographers, their attention drawn to mysterious details, struggle to locate the narratives that would accommodate them. In *Rear Window,* the *donnée* resembles many of

Hopper's paintings: a glimpse through an open apartment window that reveals the fragment of a story (see, for example, *Hopper's Night Windows*, 1928). In *Blow-Up*, an allegory of "electronic thinking," the solution is withheld as the hero is left to try out different explanations for the events that have intrigued him.

In his essay "*Longtemps, je me suis couché de bonne heure . . .*," Barthes suggests that Proust, at the beginning of his career, had hesitated "between two 'ways' he does not yet know could converge . . . the way of the Essay (of Criticism) and the way of the novel":

> Proust's hesitation . . . corresponds to a structural alternation. . . . Metaphor sustains any discourse which asks: "What is it? What does it mean?"—the real question of the Essay. Metonymy, on the contrary, asks another question: "What can follow what I say? What can be engendered by the episode I am telling?"; this is the novel's question. . . . Proust is a divided subject. . . . he knows that each incident in life can give rise either to a commentary (an interpretation) or to an affabulation which produces or imagines the narrative *before* and *after;* to interpret is to take the Critical path, to argue theory . . . to think incidents and impressions, to describe their developments, is on the contrary, to weave a Narrative.[24]

Barthes proposed in this, one of his last writings, that contemporary thinking was moving toward Proust's hybrid, a combination of the Essay's "What does it mean?" and the Novel's "What might come before or after this incident?" Godard once called this hybrid "research in the form of a spectacle," and it seems increasingly to have become the form of thinking enabled by electronic technology.[25] Despite his initial interest in Ashcan realism, Hopper seems to have grown aware that by structuring his images to imply narratives, he could intensify his depictions of everyday life. In fact, he had intuited the role that spectacle would occupy in electronic thinking, posited by Ong as a "secondary orality," again dependent on the oral historian's fundamental resources: images and stories. Hopper's paintings, with their invitations to both the question of the Essay and the question of the Novel, anticipate this development, and in doing so, they suggest that photography (and the movies) can prompt art in more ways than are dreamt of in abstraction's philosophy.

8 The Riddle of Elvis-the-Actor

As a topic, nothing could seem less promising than "Elvis the actor." Admittedly, that situation probably has less to do with Elvis's own contributions to his movies than with the films themselves, most of them specious, formulaic representations of what the pre-rock generation of producers, writers, and directors who made them thought was "youth culture." And so far, even the film studies establishment has refrained from analyses of *mise-en-scène* in *Paradise Hawaiian Style*, camera movement in *It Happened at the World's Fair*, or montage in *Double Trouble*.

At its most negative, writing about Elvis's film career also blames him. In his influential, highly opinionated *Biographical Dictionary of Film*, David Thomson writes:

There is a tradition of singers who made a string of movies because of their proven following. But is there a greater contrast between energy and routine than that between Elvis Presley the phenomenon, live and on record, and Presley the automaton on film?[1]

I want to suggest, however, that the blame lies with the failure to recognize in Elvis the beginnings of a new way of thinking about acting, and this new attitude toward performance appears from the start in his singing.

The similarities between acting and singing were often invoked in articles analyzing the extraordinary effect of Frank Sinatra. "Sinatra approached song as drama," John Lahr wrote in the *New Yorker,* echoing Julius LaRosa's tribute that Sinatra "turned a 32-bar song into a three-act play," making the listener hear and feel the story being told. Sinatra himself often spoke of singing as a kind of acting: "You begin to learn to use the lyrics of a song as a script, a scene," he confessed. "I try to transpose my thoughts about the song into a person who might be singing those words to somebody else."[2] These terms, this vocabulary help explain such spellbinding Sinatra performances as "Here's That Rainy Day," "In the Wee Small Hours of the Morning," or "You Go to My Head," where the recordings seem like episodes from longer narratives, whose beginnings and endings have been perhaps deliberately mislaid. But did Elvis-the-singer use the same acting techniques as Sinatra?

Discussions of acting usually turn on some basic oppositions:

film acting	theater acting
stars	character actors
non-naturalistic acting	naturalistic acting

Applying these terms to Sinatra and Elvis will help solve the riddle of how so charismatic a musical performer as Elvis could have had such an indifferent career in the movies.

1. Film Acting vs. Theater Acting

If you don't think that these two modes require very different things, you only have to reflect that while the greatest stage actor of the century, Laurence Olivier, never had a really important film career—and, in fact, often looked downright silly on the screen—someone with very rudimentary acting skills became the biggest movie star of all time: John Wayne. The standard way of understanding this dilemma involves the distinction between a theatrical actor's need to disappear into a role vs. the movie star's responsibility to "play himself." Film stars, in fact, have always been less actors than personalities, paid to personify (rather than impersonate) a certain character type. As one film historian (Ronald L. Davis) has written, "Most of the old studio stars created a persona, and they acted that persona no matter what role they played. Audiences flocked to the theaters more to see their favorite stars than to watch realistic performances. . . . Most of the great Hollywood stars were almost pure personality, like Clark Gable, who didn't much like acting."[3] Very rarely, a Hollywood character actor can become a star, not by displaying a consistent, distinct personality, but by impersonating, like a stage actor, various roles: Lon Chaney and Dustin Hoffman are two obvious example. But in general, the commercial cinema saved its biggest rewards for men and women who, by theatrical standards, didn't much act at all.

How does this opposition apply to singers? The most famous pop singers resemble movie stars: think of Louis Armstrong—instantly recognizable, subordinating almost every song to his own brilliant, relatively inflexible persona. Popular music's greatest character actor is probably the Ella Fitzgerald of the *Song Book* series, where her modest interpretations of Rodgers and Hart, Gershwin, Porter, Ellington, Berlin, Arlen, and Mercer seem as transparent as a newly shined window that lets the songs simply appear, almost without their having been "performed" at all. Sinatra's greatness may have something to do with his straddling this apparently irreconcilable divide: as a singer, he was at once distinctive and modest, a star giving himself up to the song as a stage actor would to a part. Sinatra's famous comeback began with a character part, the role of Maggio in *From Here to Eternity*, and his singing, although always recognizable, seemed inflected by a character actor's willingness to assume different roles.

While Elvis has moments when his persona yields to the needs of a particular song (especially in ballads), as a singer he was almost always the equivalent of a studio-era movie star, possessed of a presence so distinctive, so consistent, and so charismatic that he became, with Louis Armstrong, one of the two most parodied of all pop musicians. (The sign that Ella Fitzgerald had more in common with a stage or character actor is that she was never the subject of impressionists.) Given that persona, any filmmaking practice that sought to "lose Elvis in a role," or, in other words, to use a star as a character actor, was always wrongheaded, like asking Garbo to play a charwoman or a part written for Eve Arden.

2. Non-Naturalistic Acting vs. Naturalistic Acting

While the movie star/stage actor, star/character actor oppositions help us place Elvis as a singer, the division between non-naturalistic and naturalistic acting is even more important for understanding Elvis as a singer. Silent-film acting had two traditions, both inherited from the theater, both surviving into the present:

1. The first, which most people think of when they think of "silent-movie acting," was non-naturalistic, using broad, conventionalized gestures (the pop

eyes to indicate surprise, the bowed head to indicate grief). This style derived from the Italian *commedia dell'arte* and its descendant, Victorian melodrama. Its theoretician was a nineteenth-century French drama teacher, François Delsarte, who codified in his textbook a set of gestures designed to denote unambiguously certain moral and emotional states.[4]

With their distinctive, highly individualized appearances, movie stars, by definition, were Delsarteans. Actors such as Cary Grant, John Wayne, Katharine Hepburn, Bette Davis, and Greta Garbo almost always transcended their particular roles, reminding audiences of other moments outside the story they were watching—other movies, other posters, other magazine articles. Thus, paradoxically, for all of Hollywood's apparent commitment to realism, its reliance on bigger-than-life stars made the movies more like vaudeville than Ibsen's slice-of-life plays.

In popular music, the Delsartean gestures survived well into the twentieth century, appearing, for example, in Al Jolson's famous version of "Mammy" and "Swanee." And when soul performers Jackie Wilson and James Brown dropped to their knees to suggest that their songs' subject matter had overwhelmed them, they were simply practicing a late, slightly parodic version of Delsarte's faith that a language of gestures could convey inner feelings.

With his ever-present fedora, trench coat, cigarette, and glass of whiskey, Sinatra-the-singer was a practicing Delsartean, having borrowed this particular costume from Bogart, whom he admired and of whose Rat Pack he assumed the leadership. Elvis, too, relied on exterior codes, especially those derived from black culture (the zoot suit, the hip shaking), but as a white man, these gestures never seemed designed to convey some inner state. If Sinatra's clothes, props, and gestures often denoted a profound, sophisticated melancholy, Elvis's seemed to stand only for Elvis himself as a new possibility.

2. Silent film's other acting tradition rejected Delsarte's codified gestures, preferring a more naturalistic, subtle style premised on the psychological interiority of realistic theater. The coming of sound caused this tradition to flourish (and Delsartean grand gestures to seem immediately dated), and the equivalent transition in singing, enabled by the microphone, is marked by Jolson's grandiloquence giving way to Bing Crosby's crooning. If in retrospect Jolson seems to be shouting, Crosby, like his contemporary Fred Astaire, blurred the line between singing and ordinary speech, or at least made it difficult to detect exactly when the line had been crossed.

This tradition of realistic acting had its various branches, most prominently Stanislavski's, which eventually produced the Method. Method Acting is a misnomer, since the system taught by Lee Strasberg at New York's famous Actor's Studio was, in fact, a rehearsal method rather than a performance style. The Method taught its pupils to use "affective memories" to get inside a role:

if you needed to cry in a scene, you thought about the day your own mother had died and used that memory to bring on the required tears. The Method also encouraged research, so the studio's most famous pupil, Marlon Brando, prepared for his role as a paraplegic veteran in *The Men* by living for weeks in a wheelchair.

In such movies as *From Here to Eternity* and *The Man with the Golden Arm*, Sinatra became a method actor, abandoning the more Delsartean gestures of his earlier musical roles in *Anchors Away* and *On the Town*. As a singer, he also worked like a method actor, conveying a tortured interiority whose role was outlined by his songs' often anguished lyrics: "In the wee small hours of the morning, when the whole wide world is fast asleep, you lie awake and you think about the girl . . . "

When Elvis was introduced to David Weisbart, *Love Me Tender*'s producer, he dropped to his knees and began to recite entire passages of James Dean's dialogue from *Rebel without a Cause,* his favorite movie, which Weisbart had also produced. Elvis worshiped Dean and at one point in the 1950s was even considered for the part of Dean in a biographical movie that never got made. Dean, of course, was one of the Method's most famous products, as were Elvis's other Hollywood idols, Brando, Richard Widmark, and Rod Steiger. But unlike Sinatra, Elvis as a singer was never a method actor. In some ways, of course, the comparison is unfair. If, as Sinatra suggested, a singer's part, his script, is primarily the lyric, then Sinatra had by far the richer roles.[5] As he reached his musical peak in the mid-1950s, Sinatra entered his forties, perfectly suited to the complex, detailed, adult lyrics of the great generation of Tin Pan Alley and Broadway songwriters who had preceded him. At his musical peak, also in the mid-1950s, Elvis was twenty years younger, and his songs, after the initial mysteries of the blues (especially "Mystery Train"), were often novelty tunes aimed at adolescents ("I Got Stung"). Elvis, of course, turned even dross into gold, but he could not do so by approaching singing with the Method Acting style that Sinatra brought to songs. While Sinatra's introverted intensity perfectly matched such lines as "It seems we've stood and talked like this before. We looked at each other in the same way then, but I can't remember where or when," Elvis would have seemed ridiculous approaching his material in the same way; "A-well-a, bless my soul, what's wrong with me? I'm itching like a man on a fuzzy tree" makes a great song, but not one sung à la James Dean.

What, then, was Elvis up to? For one thing, he realized, as every great singer has, that songs are not just words, and he threw away those that didn't amount to much in the first place, slurring them, bubbling them, turning them into rhythm. But was he an actor when he was singing? In his definitive book *Acting in the Cinema,* James Naremore points out that all naturalistic acting, especially method acting, regarded performance as an outgrowth of the actor's essential self. The Method's tricks, after all, existed to enable the actor to plumb that self for the sake of the part. Sinatra's singing matches that description, most famously in his heartrending "I'm a Fool to Want You," a performance prompted by his breakup with Ava Gardner. Elvis, however, reversed that process. Instead of deriving his singing performances from some preexisting inner self (could "Mystery Train," for example, be traced to some particular experience, some particular "affective memory"?), Elvis treated the self as an effect of performance, as the result of role-playing.[6] In fact, the closest equivalent to Elvis-as-singer, which is to say Elvis-as-actor, is the moment in Godard's *Breathless* when Michel Poiccard, confronting Bogart's face on a movie poster, does his own version of Bogart's gestures. As a character, Michel results from his imitation of Bogart, his desire for a life like those in American film noirs. As a singer, Elvis was always an actor whose favorite roles included the Dean Martin–crooner and the black rhythm-and-blues shouter (especially influenced by Clyde McPhatter). In a sense, he had no self apart from these roles, a suggestion confirmed by his sometimes slavish copying of the demos sent to him.

With this skepticism about "the inner self," Elvis had intuitively anticipated postmodernism's emphasis on role-playing. But he had also outrun Hollywood's creaky film industry. He couldn't succeed in classical studio filmmaking because his acting style, unlike Sinatra's, represented the beginnings of a new tradition. In fact, he would have perfectly suited Godard's approach to filmmaking, and now, at the century's end, when we dream of imaginary artworks, we should think of a lost Godard film, a sequel perhaps to *Masculine-Feminine*, with Elvis in—what else?—the hero's role.

9 The Two Cities and the Archive: Notes on Godard

1. Two Cities

We could begin with a history lesson in the form of a conjecture. Let us imagine two cities, separated by a great distance, less by geography than by the passing of time. In the first city, by means of constant vigilance, conducted with great effort, the distinction between truth and fiction is maintained. Indeed, in this city, if a storyteller appears, one who specializes in that particular kind of tale whose existence depends on the imagination, he will be led forthwith to the city gates and put on the road to the next town. In this city, the law holds that only the truth may be spoken or told or remembered. Occasionally, tribunals convene to make decisions about when certain summaries of great events of the past have crossed an invisible line and, by leaving too much out or by putting too much in, have left the protected zone of truth for the contraband domain of fiction. Increasingly, these tribunals become more frequent and their members more powerful. Attempting to eliminate the need for this continual *ad hoc* adjudication, they call upon the city's leaders to draft rules that would distinguish, in principle, between the allowed and the forbidden, the true and the fictional. When formulated, these rules enable both the tribunes and the educated laity to detect improper arguments, contaminated by either illogic or imagination. The city leaders call these rules "rhetoric."

In the second city, at a later date, this founding opposition has been abandoned. There, the citizens make no distinction between the real and the imaginary, attending only to the consequences resulting from any event. The air seems less clear, no longer cleansed by freshening winds off the sea, left increasingly dense, as if cluttered by the stories that pile up, immune from the possibility of censure or ridicule. And yet, an odd liveliness has appeared, a charge of sensations curiously absent from the experience of those who have remained behind in the first city.

These two cities have names. Plato called the first the Republic, and he himself, in the book of that name, proposed that storytellers indulging in fiction be led to the gates. The second city developed only a hundred years ago, when it was discovered by Freud and named the Unconscious. In his famous letter to Fliess, acknowledging the failure of his theory linking hysteria to familial sexual abuse, Freud provided the city's charter: "there are no indications of reality in the unconscious, so that one cannot distinguish between the truth and fiction that is cathected with affect."[1]

We now live in this second city, subject less to the laws of Plato than to those of Freud: cathexis, overdetermination, condensation, displacement, the logic of dreams. This second city has invented its own forms of writing and telling stories, forms unrecognizable by the standards of the Republic. The first, provisional name for this new form of writing, one already being left behind for other terms, was "the cinema."

2. A Story

Here is a story. As a child, Jean-Luc Godard traveled regularly between Switzerland, his mother's family home, and France, his father's country. In May 1940, when he was nine years old, Godard was trapped in Paris when France fell to the invading Germans. To get him out of the occupied capital, his relatives sent him that autumn to Rennes, in Brittany, where he attended school. By early 1941, his family managed to return him to Nyon, a town outside of Geneva, where his father was practicing medicine. But in early November, the Germans, already thinking about defending against a possible British counterattack, moved troops into Normandy and Brittany and conducted immediate reprisals against any Frenchmen not complying with Wehrmacht demands. In the third week, a reprisal took place in the Rennes neighborhood where the nine-year-old Godard was staying. He was returning from an after-school soccer game when he heard gunshots. He hid in tall grass, separated from the main road by a railroad track. It had rained that day, and he remembers that the grass was still wet and that the wind had risen since the game and was blowing in the trees' few remaining leaves. He waited until the shooting had stopped, and after another half-hour (he was cautious), he emerged from hiding and walked toward the railroad track. He had started for home when he noticed a woman's body across the rails. She was dead, having been shot at least twice, once apparently at point-blank range. As an adult, Godard would remember that although the weather had grown cold some weeks before, the young woman was still wearing a plaid, cotton, summer dress. He had never seen her before, but then he was new to the region. What he remembered about her features he could not have said, at least not in response to any formal interrogation. In fact, he recalls, it was only years later, when he encountered those features again, particularly the boyishly cropped blonde hair, that he remembered the woman on the tracks and realized why he wanted the living woman he had seen in Preminger's *Saint Joan* and *Bonjour Tristesse,* Jean Seberg, to star in his own first feature.

3. "The Reality Effect"

In the Republic, whose boundaries gradually extended to include the Western world, the rules of rhetoric for a time enabled a citizen to segregate documentary from fiction. But as Scholes and Kellogg describe in *The Nature of Narrative,* the two great branches of narrative, the empirical and the fictional, began to combine during the Renaissance in a synthesis that appeared "at least as early as Boccaccio" and masterfully in Cervantes.[2] The novel, of course, emerged precisely as "a product of the reunion of the empirical and fictional," as writers developed means of obscuring the distinction between them. Thus, by 1719, one could begin a story by scattering just those details whose simultaneous referential precision and narrative irrelevance Barthes would later designate as the principal sources of "the reality effect":[3]

> I was born in the Year 1632, in the City of York, of a good Family, tho' not of that Country, my Father being a Foreigner of Bremen, who settled first at *Hull:* He got a good Estate by Merchandise, and leaving off his Trade, lived afterward at York, from whence he had married my Mother, whose Relations were named Robinson. . . .
> I had two elder Brothers, one of whom was Lieutenant Collonel to an En-

glish Regiment of Foot in Flanders, formerly commanded by the famous Coll. Lockhart, and was killed at the Battle near Dunkirk against the Spaniards. What became of my second Brother I never knew. . . . [4]

The story I told about Godard, for example, which I imagined, depends on these same devices: the specific dates and places, the incidental details, the mingling of the empirical with the fictional. By now, the strategies have become so familiar that one is on guard against them. But the advent of photography upped the ante, dramatically increasing the difficulty in distinguishing the fictive from the real. Surely it is no accident that only two years after identifying as the source of literature's "reality effect" those superfluous details providing "insignificant notation" Barthes renamed them "the third meaning" and proposed such signifiers without signifieds as the essence of the photographic image.[5]

Barthes's earlier essay, "The Reality Effect," provided the basis for semiotic dissections of purportedly fictional material. That piece's implications turned on equating aesthetic realism with a loss of control. If obviously symbolic or narratively pregnant details alerted you to a writing's fictional status, that signal depended on the well-established sense of reality's messiness, its refusal to conform neatly to storytelling's demands. Thus, no reader would ever mistake the villa of Triste-le-Roy (in Borges's "Death and the Compass") for anything but a literary contrivance, with its "pointless symmetries" and "maniacal repetitions," where "one balcony was reflected in another balcony" and "double stairways led to double balustrades."[6] On the other hand, the apparent *pointlessness* of the details Barthes signals out from "A Simple Heart"— "an old piano supported, under a barometer, a pyramidal heap of boxes and cartons"—produce the reality effect because their narrative inefficiency implies Flaubert's inability to square the world to his plot.

Thus, two equations:

signs of order or control = art
signs of disorder or loss of control = reality

But anyone who has seen *Citizen Kane*'s newsreel opening, with its jump cuts, scratched film stock, and unprivileged camera positions, knows how easily any filmmaker can fake signs of disorder. In fact, at this stage of photography and cinema and video, what exactly *are* the codes? For some time, for example, I have been interested in the three images reproduced here as figures 15 through 17. Once, I showed them to colleagues of mine in the music department at Florida, asking them to indicate which were "real" and which were "fictional." In figure 15, the woman's looking back into the camera indicates, one replied, an obvious staging; hence, that image is fictional. But we know, from Noël

15. *Les Vampires*

Burch's *Correction Please* (among others), that because the diegetic effect depends upon our sense of an onscreen event's independent status (which the camera just happens to record), fiction filmmakers almost immediately forbade the direct gaze into the camera, relegating it to comedy and documentary. Thus, the woman's look, by this logic, suggests the *opposite* of fiction.

Figure 16, however, with its melodramatic lighting, its potentially symbolic arch, its anachronistic trolley, and its silhouetted woman—the image's obvious design, implying any number of Sternbergian plots—indicates fiction. As does something about figure 17, perhaps the sense, generated by the pose of the flag waver or the curve of the road or the wind in the trees, that this exact moment represents a story's climax.

But the first image comes from a fiction film, Feuillade's *Les Vampires*, while the latter two (the first from Josef Sudek, the second from Jacques Lartigue) do not. With photographs, as so many people have shown, the crucial distinction between fiction and documentary becomes increasingly difficult to maintain.

Why? Because, as Walter Benjamin first intuited and Jean Baudrillard has explained, photography (and, by implication, the cinema) represents a rupture in the history of representation, replacing that Platonic notion (which always implies a referent against which an image can be verified) with the new experience of "simulation." In this situation of "hyperreality," where images have real effects and have thus become indistinguishable from "the real," a term that loses its meaning, "referential value is nullified," as Baudrillard puts it, and "total relativity" replaces it. In this realm, "signs will exchange among themselves exclusively" in "combinatory play." Thus, all semiotic attempts to distinguish the fictional from the real become hopeless, Platonic anachronisms, for as Baudrillard summarizes, "The era of simulation is thus every-

16. Josef Sudek

17. Lartigue

where initiated by the interchangeability of previously contradictory or dialectically opposed terms."[7]

Not coincidentally, this Baudrillardian vision conforms precisely to the Freudian paradigm. For psychoanalysis not only posits the indistinguishability of real and imagined events, it proposes that the historical accuracy of the analyst's explanation matters less than its narrative appeal. As Donald Spence has shown in his *Narrative Truth and Historical Truth: Meaning and Interpretation in Psychoanalysis,* "interpretations are persuasive [and therapeutic] not because of their evidentiary value but because of their rhetorical appeal; conviction emerges because the fit is good, not because we have necessarily made contact with the past."[8]

When we remember that in "The Third Meaning," Barthes identified the filmic's essence in such things as a courtier's eyebrow or an old woman's scarf, and that in psychoanalysis, Freud located the patient's cure in such individualized symptoms as a dream about wolves or a fear of butterflies, we see confirmed Baudrillard's point that the first effect of hyperreality, the realm of simulations, is the vertigo of the detail.

4. Godard

Beginning his career during television's first decade, Godard anticipated the hyperreality to come, with its attendant collapse of the documentary-fiction distinction. Two out of his first three features, *Breathless* and *A Woman Is a Woman,* now seem exactly Freudian, with their plots demonstrating how imagined images ("Bogart" and MGM musicals) have actual consequences. His interviews at the time contain the justifiably famous remarks:

[Of Angela in *A Woman Is a Woman*] She does not distinguish between documentary and fiction. Just like me.

Cinema, Truffaut said, is spectacle—Méliès—and research—Lumière. If I analyse myself today, I see that I have always wanted, basically, to do research in the form of a spectacle. The documentary side is: a man in a particular situation. The spectacle comes when one makes this man a gangster or a secret agent.

reportage is interesting only when placed in a fictional context, but fiction is interesting only if it is validated by a documentary context.

The *Nouvelle Vague,* in fact, may be defined in part by this new relationship between fiction and reality. . . .

A distinction is usually drawn between Lumière and Méliès. Lumière, they say, is documentary, and Méliès is fantasy. But today, what do we see when we watch their films? We see Méliès filming the reception of the King of Yugoslavia by the

President of the Republic. A newsreel, in other words. And at the same time we find Lumière filming a family card game in the *Bouvard and Pécuchet* manner. In other words, fiction.

Let us be more precise and say that what interested Méliès was the ordinary in the extraordinary; and Lumière, the extraordinary in the ordinary.[9]

[*Breathless*] is really a documentary on Jean Seberg and Jean-Paul Belmondo.[10]

As a filmmaker, Godard set out to practice the hybrid form he described in his interviews. In *Breathless, A Woman Is a Woman,* and *Vivre sa Vie,* documentary material repeatedly intrudes upon the fictional diegesis. Sometimes Godard pans or cuts away from his characters to reveal the ordinary world going on with its business. At times, as when Belmondo and Seberg stroll down a Parisian boulevard, documentary enters at the margins of the frame.

5. Proust's "Third Way" and Freud's "Signorelli"

Why did Godard, and to a certain extent the other New Wave directors, choose this way of working? What immediately occasioned the emergence of this fiction-documentary hybrid? As Truffaut so famously announced, the new film-making would break with the French film industry's "tradition of quality," those big-budget, scriptwriter-dominated, literary adaptations that seemed so hermetically sealed off from contemporary experience. *La Politique des Auteurs* would equate filmmaking with writing, and directors with poets and novelists. But although the *Nouvelle Vague* would draw on both traditionally romantic notions of literary self-expression and Sartre's existentialist calls for responsibility, it needed a distinctive form. Most of the New Wave filmmakers had apprenticed in short, low-budget documentaries, but the hybrid in which they did their best work had a tradition in French literature, in Sartre, of course, but especially in Proust.

In a 1978 lecture at the *Collège de France,* in which he announced his own desire for "a new practice of writing," Barthes returned, as he had so many times, to Proust's example, and in particular, to Proust's early hesitation between two modes:

Proust [Barthes writes] seems to be at the intersection of two paths, two genres, torn between two "ways" he does not yet know could converge . . . : the way of the Essay (of Criticism) and the way of the Novel. . . .

I should point out that Proust's hesitation . . . corresponds to a structural alternation: the two "ways" he hesitates between are the two terms of an opposition articulated by Jakobson: that of Metaphor and Metonymy. Metaphor sustains any discourse which asks: "What is it? What does it mean?—the real question of the essay [and, we might say in passing, of the documentary]. Metonymy, on the contrary, asks another question: "What can follow what I say? What can be engendered by the episode I am telling?": this is the Novel's question. . . . Proust is a divided subject . . . ; he knows that each incident in life can give rise either to a commentary (an interpretation) or to an affabulation which produces or imagines the narrative *before* and *after:* to interpret is to take the Critical path, to argue theory; to think incidents and impressions, to describe their developments, is on the contrary to weave a Narrative. . . . [11]

Proust, Barthes proposed, had developed *a third form,* "neither Essay nor Novel," but one whose structure became "rhapsodic," a mode in which "pieces, fragments are subject to certain correspondences, arrangements, reappearances." This rhapsodic structure resembles both Freudian dream logic and cinematic editing practices, especially those identified with Eisenstein's "cinema of attractions." In these cases, we might imagine a monitor attached to three knobs, representing the three registers Bill Nichols identifies in *Ideology and the Image:* the poetic, the expository, and the narrative.[12] Further imagine that by dialing these knobs, one might change their relative prominence. Thus, Hollywood Cinema, the most prominent fiction filmmaking, turns up the narrative knob at the expense of the expository and poetic ones. Traditional documentary filmmaking turns up the expository. Freud suggests, however, that the Unconscious, while hinting at narration and exposition, runs almost entirely in the poetic register, making associative leaps by means of such devices as rhymes, shapes, and puns. In this register, pattern similarity supersedes narrative or expository logic as a means of getting from one thing to another, and the capacity of "Botticelli" and "Boltraffio" to replace "Signorelli" results from, among other accidents of language, the slide from "Herr" to "Signor."[13] The Unconscious, in other words, amounts to Baudrillard's hyperreality, where "the structural dimension . . . gains autonomy, to the exclusion of the referential dimension. . . . from now on signs will interchange among themselves exclusively, without interacting with the real."[14]

This combinatory logic is precisely cinematic, particularly resembling Eisenstein's "attractions" editing, which attended to autonomous details, used less for their narrative or expository possibilities than for their poetic function. Noël Burch describes this strategy:

In the peace and quiet of the cutting room, the editor has always been the first to reflect on the extraordinary variety of material that the world of chance, once captured on film, provides him. . . . Even in the case of the most meticulously "staged" films, the editor will soon notice that minor accidents completely beyond the control of the director, who was not able even to see them during the shooting, have given him an opportunity to create a very strong articulation be-

tween shots. . . . The accidental in fact provides far more subtle and more complex cutting possibilities than any film-maker can foresee. . . . In the scene in
October where the buxom bourgeois women in their rustling laces poke out the
young sailor's eyes with the tips of their umbrellas, Eisenstein brings the camera
right up to the action and follows it very closely, aware that, in addition to the
intrinsic beauty of the shots thus obtained, this kaleidoscopic flurry of dancing
silhouettes, whirling cloth, and dripping blood will result in a cascade of images,
visible in all their detail only in the developed film, . . . (a feather boa visible on
screen for a few fractions of a second, a flare frame only a few inches long), aware
that these "accidents" will later afford him the possibility of cutting to another
shot in a visually interesting way at almost any frame.[15]

6. The Archive

The move from the Republic to the Unconscious involves the replacement of
traditional rhetoric with dream logic. While Baudrillard's suggestion that "the
era of simulation" initiates the conflation of previously opposed terms would
account for the increasing intermingling of fiction and documentary, it would
not entirely explain Godard's hybrid filmmaking. Godard, after all, came of
age intellectually in the 1950s, before hyperreality had become widespread.
How did Godard imagine his new form?

Perhaps the most important of the prerequisites for the French New Wave
was the *Cinémathèque*—the archive.[16] Our word "archive" comes from the
Greek *arkhé*, meaning "government." That word also provides the root for "archaeology," the science of the archive. We know, of course, that Foucault, especially in his early writings, referred to himself as "an archaeologist." But the
other person who thought of himself as an archaeologist was Freud, who kept
archaeological objects, particularly Egyptian ones, on his desk. The metaphor
at first seems obvious: the necessity of "digging" into the past (of a civilization or a patient). More important, however, the metaphor suggests the *simul-
taneity* of the past and present in the unconscious of the patient, where events
from the past, mingling and combining with those from the present, influence
and determine behavior.

The *Cinémathèque* is *the unconscious of the medium.* Any part of it can be
activated at any time, and any part of it can combine with any other part (as
Godard will show: *A Woman Is a Woman* as a "neorealist musical"). As if prescient about Foucault's diagnosis of the archive's relation to power, to questions of who can speak, whose utterances will be preserved, whose will be revived, *Cinémathèque* boss Henri Langlois, *at the saving stage,* tried to be as
nonjudgmental as possible: his rule was simple—*save everything* (which has
become the new model for curatorship). He limited his role to determining

the combinations (often suggestive) in which films would be revived and screened.

The odd combinations of Langlois's programs, the mixture of genres, of modes, of periods, of quality, derive from the Surrealists' habits of filmwatching and filmmaking, both of which emphasized disruption, discontinuity, and surprise. If Breton made it a habit to go from theater to theater without knowing the program or the schedule, if he insisted on leaving as soon as he began to understand what was going on, if he encouraged appropriation and collage, the *Cinémathèque* merely translated those policies into an exhibition practice.

Confronted by this hodgepodge of movies, the *Cahiers* group resembled Freud encountering his patients' unconsciouses. How did they make sense of what they saw? We are, in fact, looking for the principles of transformation that would guide us in using the archives whose ubiquity now constitutes one of postmodernity's basic features. Freud posits that the unconscious constitutes the archive of the patient. To solve problems (wishes, anxieties, needs), you summon this material the way you go to a library to do research on a problem. The unconscious, Freud proposed, amounts to a system of scanning and experimentation whereby certain combinations get tried out.

The mechanisms, Freud wrote, are reducible to two: condensation and displacement. Thus, in the Signorelli incident, all the fears about death and sex, all the stories about the Turks and Freud's suicidal patients get compressed into a few names, but the issue itself is displaced into the safer realm of forgetting the name of an Italian Renaissance painter.

If we take *Breathless* as an activation of the archive (the unconsciously stored material from years of filmwatching), we can see that the movie works precisely by *condensation* (all the gangster stories, Bogart movies, documentaries, neorealist films such as *Open City)* and *displacement* (from the United States to France, from a pure crime story to one mixed with existentialism and self-referentiality, to another kind of filmmaking altogether). *Breathless,* in other words, condenses *The Killer Is Loose* with *Open City,* using the details that the two films share, while displacing both from their original purposes.

Compare, for example, the scene from *Open City* when Anna Magnani is killed to the beginning of *The Killer Is Loose.* What is the point of resemblance, the means of condensation? They both take place on the street, they both are shot in documentary style, with available lighting and fast film stock: thus, they can be combined and used, but for other purposes.

This combination, this hybrid of fiction and documentary amounts to Godard's version of what Barthes called Proust's "third way." It mixes the essayist mode of metaphor with the novelistic mode of metonymy. And when we think that metonymy/displacement and narration look for places where two systems diverge, we see that in activating the *Cinémathèque's* archive,

18. Still from *Open City*

20. Still from *The Killer Is Loose*

19. Still from *Breathless*

21. Still from *Breathless*

Godard was practicing the two forms of cinematic editing that he had celebrated as a critic and between which he would alternate as a filmmaker: (1)
Hollywood's continuity mode, whose basic principle of matching works to
discover the points of coincidence between two shots—their locus of potential
condensation; and (2) Soviet Montage, whose principles of discontinuity and
shock amount to a strategy of sustained *displacement.* As a critic, Godard
never seemed satisfied with the opposition, coined by Bazin, of montage vs.
mise-en-scène, Eisenstein vs. Renoir. He wanted it both ways, and by using
dream logic to combine fiction and documentary, he bridged film history's
great divide.

When you talk about the media today, one question con-
stantly recurs: Do the new media wipe out the old?
—Walter J. Ong[1]
When you get right down to it, the most fantastic thing
you could film is people reading.
—Jean-Luc Godard[2]

10 Film and Literature

Although few people writing about "Film and Literature" have acknowledged
it, a single question haunts this area of media studies: why has this topic, obviously central to humanities-based film education, prompted so little distinguished work? In 1975, Louis D. Giannetti did manage to propose that "the
overwhelming bulk of what's been written about the relationship of film and
literature is open to serious question";[3] twenty-five years later, however, even
that judgment seems generous, with its implication that such books as George
Bluestone's *Novels into Film* and Robert Richardson's *Literature and Film*
would demand (and ultimately receive) a series of vigorous responses.[4] Instead, contemporary film studies has simply ignored these books, dismissing
them as completely as modern scientists have pre-Newtonian physics. And, indeed, if a practicing physicist perforce regards as irrelevant to his own work
Aristotle's theory of motion, what must a film semiotician or poststructuralist

make of Richardson's chapter-length analysis of Eliot's *Waste Land* and Fellini's *La Dolce Vita* as modern reworkings of *Ecclesiastes*' theme, "the emptiness of life"?[5] Thus, throughout much of the 1980s and 1990s, "Film and Literature" fell into thorough disrepute, as if the sensed inadequacies of the topic's principal books, journals, and textbooks had somehow discredited the subject itself.[6] How did this situation arise? Answering that question should tell us something not only about film and literature, but also about the apparatuses[7] under which both have been taught.

Like any historical formation, Film and Literature as a topic is overdetermined. In other words, if we want to know why it took the direction it did, we need to look at the factors that influenced its development, in particular, from the most general to the most immediate: (1) the nature of narrative, (2) the norm of cinema, (3) the methods of academic literary and film study, and (4) the exigencies of the academic profession. Each of these factors has shaped the writing and teaching that have gone under the rubric "Film and Literature."

The Nature of Narrative

If from the early days of film criticism, the cinema invited comparisons with literature (rather than with music, sculpture, architecture, or painting), the reason was obvious: both were narratives. (In fact, "Film and Literature" has always meant Film and the Novel, or Film and Drama, but never Film and Poetry, unless the poetry under consideration tells a story.) Theoretical work in narratology, the study of narrative wherever it may be found, legitimized that comparison, demonstrating that as a means of organizing information, narrative is not specific to any one medium.[8] Since literature departments were traditionally charged with the responsibility for narrative, they inevitably appropriated for study this powerful new means of actualizing it—the movies. In doing so, however, these departments neglected to ask two questions that now seem crucial: first, do popular narratives differ in some fundamental way from "artistic," "high-art" ones; and second, why had the cinema committed itself almost exclusively to storytelling? These questions went unaddressed as critics contented themselves with interminable analyses of individual cases, comparisons between novels and their filmed versions. In retrospect, the two overlooked questions seem to hold the key to the Film/Literature comparison, and the failure to take them up almost certainly accounts for the dead end in which the field quickly found itself.

Of all academics, Film and Literature scholars should have been the best situated to spot the first question's significance. With the whole enterprise of Film and Literature founded on the hypothesis of narrative transmutability, they might have seen that stories (and popular stories in particular) depend for their legibility on codes, conventions, connotations, *topoi*, and tropes that similarly migrate from medium to medium—in short, on an intertextuality that includes not only Film and Literature, but all the other media as well. As Roland Barthes described this process, "The cultural codes [deployed by any single story] . . . will emigrate to other texts; there is no lack of hosts."[9]

Take, for example, the scene in *Casablanca* that introduces Rick Blaine (Humphrey Bogart). After a closeup of Rick's hand boldly authorizing a check, the camera pulls back to reveal Bogart, seated in a white dinner jacket, smoking a cigarette, playing with a chess set placed next to a half-empty champagne glass. As Hollywood knew perfectly well, the immediate, efficient, shorthand characterization telegraphed by this image (a sophisticated, jaded, clever man, simultaneously proud and melancholy) derived from the objects (tuxedo, champagne glass, chess set) whose meaning had become coded through repeated, similar uses in other movies, popular fiction, advertising, comic strips, and "common sense." At its most extreme, the Hollywood system sought to codify even its leading actors, turning them into predictably signifying objects, not only through consistent cinematic use (typecasting), but also through extracinematic, semiliterary forms of publicity (press releases, fan-magazine articles, bios, interviews, and news plants).[10] Long before its critics, in other words, Hollywood recognized the perpetual interchange between film and writing and its role in creating (or controlling) meaning.

Film and Literature scholars might have spotted this interchange, too, had they noticed how popular narratives differ from the avant-garde in relying heavily on codes that are never medium-specific.[11] Their specialized literary training, however, predisposed these critics to attend only to how a work functioned within its own medium's tradition: if *Madame Bovary* could best be explained by studying Flaubert's use of the novel form, then so could a movie. But while even (especially?) avant-garde texts deploy general codes (in the process Bakhtin called "heteroglossia"),[12] they typically display a preoccupation with their own medium that popular works, aimed at nonspecialist audiences, cannot afford. Further, as *S/Z* demonstrates, avant-garde texts ("the writerly") criticize, ironize, and parody the conventions on which popular works ("the readerly") depend. Indeed, far from contesting its signifiers' received connotations, popular narratives such as *Casablanca* ratify them. To the extent that the sum of such connotations equals a culture's ideology, such ratification amounts to a political act affirming the *status quo*, and one no less important for taking place at the level of signs.

Their failure to spot popular narratives' distinctive, radical intertextuality caused Film and Literature scholars to miss an insight that was right before their eyes: if narrative was not specific to any medium, neither was ideology. Indeed, the instant accessibility of popular stories, especially the movies, depends on a signifier's connotation remaining consistent as it migrates from form to form: if a champagne glass means one thing in an ad and another in a film, *Casablanca*'s audience might not be so readily able to decipher Rick Blaine's character.

The histories of semiotic, reader-response, and structuralist accounts of the reading process (our negotiation with signs) converged in ideological criticism, a theoretical practice that the movies, a thoroughly commercial practice utterly exposed to the whims of the marketplace, have always demanded. Barthes made the semiotic/ideology connection at least as early as *Mythologies* (1957; English version, 1972), his now-classic analysis of the behavior, events, and culture of everyday life. His 1964 dissection of a French pasta ad ("The Rhetoric of the Image")[13] made this point more explicit: immediate intelligibility requires signifiers whose connotations are predictable within a culture (e.g., a champagne glass, as opposed to a beer bottle, must always suggest "sophistication"); the sum of these stock connotations equals a culture's ideology, its elaborate lexicon of representations. Understanding even a single ad, in short, requires that a reader participate (however ironically) in that lexicon whose signifiers he has necessarily encountered elsewhere.

Serious investigations of *narrative* intertextuality (and its entailing ideological disposition) began only with Barthes's *S/Z* (1970; English version, 1974). By subjecting a single Balzac novella to what he called "a slow motion reading" and by contrasting its "readerly" acceptance of convention with *Bouvard and Pecuchet*'s ambivalence, Barthes demonstrated that popular narratives not only follow the route of received ideology, they also propagate it. Such ideology is intertextual ("there is no lack of hosts"), but film and literature are especially visible sites of its traces.

Presumably familiar with both written and filmed narratives, Literature and Film scholars might have been among the first to recognize both the conventional ideological grounding of popular storytelling and its thoroughgoing intertextuality. Most, however, treated all narratives alike, simply transposing methods developed for the study of "high art" literature. Nevertheless, the few who immediately followed Barthes's lead often came from literature departments.[14] As a group, they distinguished themselves by appearing more interested in ideology and theory than in either literature or film per se. But their training in the latter two enabled them to detect the elaborate intertextual, ideological scaffolding that sustained popular fictions. Thus, while the non-literature-based film program at Wisconsin became famous for distinguished aesthetic, formalist analyses, several of Indiana's comparative literature film students went on to found *Jump Cut*, a Marxist journal that monitors the indiscriminate wanderings of ideology among the various narrative media, which now include music video.

The Norm of Cinema

Film and Literature's basic interest in how stories travel from medium to medium might have allowed the field to anticipate contemporary theory's linked concerns with narrative, intertextuality, and ideology. Sensing the importance of the second question—Why had the cinema committed itself almost exclusively to storytelling?—would have been more difficult. In fact, the overwhelmingly dominant filmmaking enterprise, Hollywood, has always worked as hard as possible to keep that question from occurring to *anyone*. Taking that effort into account, we can rephrase the question: Why was commercial filmmaking so eager to make the feature-length fictional narrative seem the inherent definition of "the cinema"? Significantly, the answer to that question involves narrative literature, in particular, its favored status among a certain filmgoing population.

As early as 1964, Marshall McLuhan suggested an answer to why movies told stories: the content of a new medium, he wrote in *Understanding Media*, is always an old medium.[15] Thus, written narratives appropriate oral tales just as the movies borrow from books and television from film. When we remember that more than half of all commercial movies derive from literature,[16] that television's basic genres (news, situation comedy, the detective story, melodrama, the Western, etc.) descend from Hollywood, and that television devotes an enormous percentage of its programming literally to replaying old movies, we may think that McLuhan has cleared up the problem.[17] But McLuhan articulated as a metaphysical principle what in fact was a historical development. There is no inherent definition of "the cinema." For specific, albeit multiple reasons, our films have been almost exclusively fictional narratives. Under different circumstances, however, they might have become primarily lyric expressions, theoretical essays, scientific investigations, vaudeville reviews, or all of these things and others besides. That they did not, of course, has everything to do with money.

Although the cinema has most often been compared to literature, it really has far more in common with architecture. Both forms are public, collaborative, and above all, expensive. In both arts, economic constraints have always dictated the shape of the work produced. In comparison, literature (especially "serious" literature) seems almost a priestly calling: novelists and poets, at least since Romanticism, have (for better or worse) been largely able to write whatever pleased them, without regard for audience or expense. At its origins, the cinema attested to divergent concerns, some similarly disinterested. While Méliès intended his films as entertainments, the Lumière brothers, as Noël Burch has argued, regarded theirs as part of the scientific research tradition

of photographers Eadweard Muybridge and Albert Londe.[18] While that tradition has survived in the documentary, both it and Méliès's stunts quickly gave
way, under commercial pressure, to what became the movies' principal form:
narrative fiction.

In a series of important essays, Burch has maintained that while primitive cinema's *presentational* mode appealed to a proletarian audience accustomed to vaudeville, melodrama, circus, puppet shows, conjuring, and street
entertainment, it did not satisfy the bourgeoisie's taste for the *representational*.
The movies could do so only by adopting the bourgeoisie's preferred arts,
the nineteenth-century realistic novel and drama, reactualized in cinema by
means of what Burch calls "the Institutional Mode of Representation," his
term for what is more commonly called "continuity" or "the invisible style."[19]
In brief, the film industry spent the twentieth century's first two decades
developing the cinematic equivalent of that seamless "writing degree zero"
that Barthes saw as the essence of realist prose fiction.[20] The resulting system,
largely in place by the early 1920s and requiring for its perfection only the final
cement of synchronous sound, turned on detailed protocols regarding shot-
to-shot matching and *mise-en-scène* centering. The result was a rhetoric so
naturalized that its traces disappeared: what appeared on the screen seemed
the work of no maker's hand. More important, the single form that the movies
had become now appeared the inevitable definition of "the cinema" whose
other possibilities were quickly forgotten.[21] This naturalized norm served another immediate purpose. As George Mitchell describes, the major film producers' tacit decision to define "the movie" as a feature-length fiction, employing stars and elaborate sets, created a drastically effective barrier-to-entry that
rapidly destroyed most independent production and established the oligopo-
listic industry we still know today.[22]

The whole enterprise of continuity rested on film's *rapprochement* with
literature, especially with narrative prose fiction, whose enigmas, forward mo-
mentum, and psychological coherence motivate, and thereby conceal, all rhetorical machinery.[23] More urgently, literature provided a young, voracious,
financially vulnerable industry with an apparently limitless supply of proved
raw material. With "embourgeoisement" and consolidation achieved, Hollywood needed to concentrate on maintaining a hold over its recently acquired
audience. Significantly, it often sought to do so, especially during box office
downturns, by upping its reliance on pre-sold product: the already successful
novel, story, Broadway play, or classic—in short, on literature.

Hollywood made its appropriation of literature's narrative mode seem inevitable. Nevertheless, in Ian Watt's 1957 *The Rise of the Novel*, Film and Literature scholars had a powerful precedent for regarding any aesthetic form as
the product of historical (particularly economic) circumstances.[24] Their fail-

ure to make this connection had to do with the prevailing paradigm of "English" and with the concrete demands of the academic profession.

The Methods of Academic Literature and Film Study

Contemporary critical theory, perhaps emulating the Frankfurt School's productive merger of Freud and Marx, has typically worked synthetically. Film critics especially seized on the discovery that the apparently natural norm of realist narrative in fact rested on an ideologically sustained network of stock, intertextual connotations. This position in turn led to the by now well-developed critique of realism as an inherently repressive mode.[25] Although their field might have given them a privileged viewpoint on these developments, Literature and Film scholars, as we have seen, did not anticipate Barthes's suggestive analyses of ideology's intertextual migrations and did not follow up on Watt's treatment of the novel as a historical formation. What *did* Literature and Film scholars do? Adaptation studies.

A look at Jeffrey Egan Welch's *Literature and Film: An Annotated Bibliography, 1909–1977*[26] will suggest the dominance of this one approach. Of 1,235 entries, the vast majority come equipped with such titles as the following:

"Hemingway on the Screen: His Universal Themes Fared Better Than His Topical Ones"
"*Macbeth:* The Making of the Film"
"Reconciliation: *Slaughterhouse-Five*—The Film and the Novel"
"Sirk's *The Tarnished Angels: Pylon* Recreated"
"Henry James into Film"
"Films and Edith Wharton"
"*Blow-Up* from Cortazar to Antonioni"
"*The Bridge on the River Kwai:* From the Novel to the Movie"
"*The Fox:* The Film and the Novel"
"Three Filmed *Hamlets*"

The sheer number of these articles, their dogged resort to the individual case study, the lack of any evidence of cumulative knowledge development or heuristic potential—all these factors suggest that as a discipline, Literature and Film largely remained in what Thomas Kuhn called a "pre-paradigmatic state."[27] Without benefit of a presiding poetics, Literature and Film scholars could only persist in asking about individual movies the same unproductive layman's question (How does the film compare to the book?), getting the same unproductive answer (The book is better). Each article seemed isolated from all the others, its insights apparently stopped at the borders of the specific film or novel selected for analysis.

Strictly speaking, however, Film and Literature was not without paradigm; for a field growing in the 1960s out of literature departments, it simply inherited the assumptions of the dominant New Criticism. But despite its paraphernalia of manifestos and scientist vocabulary, New Criticism proved ultimately antitheoretical. Its grounding in the individual critical sensibility (T. S. Eliot: "There is no method except to be very intelligent"[28]) and a reified notion of the text (to be appreciated for its "integrity," "relevance," "unity," "function," "maturity," "subtlety," "adequacy")[29] authorized only close readings of particular cases and not a more sweeping, explanatory poetics. Further, New Criticism's veneration of "art" and its famous hostility to translation ("the Heresy of Paraphrase")[30] sponsored Film and Literature's obsessive refrain that cinematic versions of literary classics failed to live up to their sources. Indeed, most of these articles could have used the same subtitle: "But Compared to the Original . . . "[31]

The inadequacy of this objection has become apparent. Philosophically, it rests on a hierarchy/opposition of *original* and *copy,* which Jacques Derrida has repeatedly deconstructed. Practically, it rests on a notion of original "aura" dissipated by what Walter Benjamin first described as modernity's rapidly accumulating tools for mechanical reproduction.[32] In Derrida's terms, any criticism that denounces the copy in the name of the original works in vain to arrest the inevitable volatility of signs:

And this is the possibility on which I want to insist: the possibility of disengagement and citational graft which belongs to the structure of every mark, spoken or written. . . . every sign, linguistic or non-linguistic, spoken or written . . . in small or large unit, can be *cited,* put between quotation marks; and in doing so it can break with every given context, engendering an infinity of new contexts in a manner which is absolutely illimitable.[33]

The film adaptation, in Derridean language, is not simply a faded imitation of a superior, authentic original: it is a "citation" grafted into a new context and thereby inevitably refunctioned. Thus, far from destroying the literary source's meaning, adaptation "disseminated" it in a process that Benjamin found democratizing:

[T]echnical reproduction can put the copy of the original into situations which would be out of reach for the original itself. Above all, it enables the original to meet the beholder halfway, be it in the form of a photograph or a phonograph record. The cathedral leaves its locale to be received in the studio of a lover of art; the choral production, performed in an auditorium or in the open air, resounds in the drawing room. . . .

One might generalize by saying: the technique of reproduction detaches the reproduced object from the domain of tradition. By making many reproductions it substitutes a plurality of copies for a unique existence. And in permitting the reproduction to meet the beholder or listener in his own particular situation, it reactivates the object reproduced. These two processes lead to a tremendous shattering of tradition. . . .

Instead of being based on ritual, it [art] begins to be based on another practice—politics.[34]

Many Literature and Film scholars, however, resisted the process that Benjamin celebrated as inescapable. Fearful of seeing literature's narrative role usurped by the movies, and under the sway of New Criticism's religious reverence for "serious art," these critics typically used the adaptation study to shore up literature's crumbling walls.

New Criticism's attempts to define the essence of "Poetry," "The Novel," and "Literature" also encouraged Film and Literature scholars to use adaptation articles as vehicles for speculating about, in Seymour Chatman's words, "What Novels Can Do That Films Can't (and Vice Versa)."[35] Such articles normally advised readers of the cinema's limitations: it had, for example, no tenses, no means of maintaining strict points-of-view, no descriptions, and no way of revealing "interior consciousness." Most of this speculation was useless, based as it was on the severely curtailed definition of "the movies" that Hollywood had successfully naturalized. Even in its reverse formulation—Eisenstein-sponsored discoveries of literary "anticipations" of some cinematic device such as montage—this whole project rested on notions of unchanging, idealist objects ("Literature," "Cinema") now thoroughly discredited.

In sum, Literature and Film scholars wrote adaptation studies because New Criticism had trained them to do so. For some reason, they did not see that the cinema's very different determinations (commercial exposure, collaborative production, public consumption) made irrelevant methods of analysis developed for "serious literature."[36] That reason has much to do with the immediate demands of the academic profession.

The Exigencies of the Academic Profession

In the spring of 1971, the Midwest Modern Language Association devoted its entire *Bulletin* to two topics: "Film and Literature" and the growing crisis in the academic job market.[37] While the MMLA obviously regarded these two subjects as discrete, hindsight has exposed their connection. The sociology of knowledge has repeatedly demonstrated that basic academic structures, normally taken for granted (having been naturalized as thoroughly as Hollywood's continuity style), materially affect such things as canon formation, choice of methodologies, and definitions of literacy.[38] In specific, Jonathan Culler has observed how professional obligations have reinforced scholars' preference for isolated close readings:

[O]ur tenure system creates a need for theories and methods that generate numerous small projects which can be completed in less than six years and listed on curriculum vitae. Since interpretation can generate an endless series of twenty-page articles, it suits our system much better than theories whose projects would take years to complete. . . . It would be interesting to investigate whether in countries with different academic reward systems many fewer interpretations are published and writing about literature takes more varied forms.[39]

"An endless series of twenty-page articles" amounts to a reasonable description of what has been produced under the rubric of Literature and Film. In asking how that situation came about, we should first remember that academic film studies began its rise precisely during the moment when the job market for Ph.D.'s in literature first fell apart—in the late 1960s and early 1970s. Obviously, film's admission into literature departments was itself motivated by an attempt to maintain declining enrollments in the humanities. For the individual job candidate, untenured assistant professor, or ambitious tenured faculty member, the rapidly escalating requirements for employment, tenure, and promotion conspired to encourage rapid and frequent publication. Restricted in scope, demanding neither sustained research into nor historical research about the two media, the typical adaptation study had things in common with that undergraduate staple, the comparison-contrast paper—it was easy to turn out, it satisfied the requirements, and it could be done over and over again. Surely it is no accident that the principal journal for such articles, *Literature/Film Quarterly*, began in 1973 as the job market worsened. Significantly (and admirably), that journal has always reserved most of its space for articles by graduate students, junior faculty, and teachers at small, relatively unprestigious colleges and universities—all obviously groups needing to publish.[40]

Coda: Possibilities for Future Work

Inevitably, all writing will return to the pictogram. It's been foretold down the century as words turned into objects, stories fell apart, and the medium became the message.
—C. Carr[41]

Twenty years ago, one of American film studies' most prominent figures, Dudley Andrew, called for a moratorium on the kind of Film and Literature article I have been describing—what Andrew referred to as "the discourse of fidelity," "unquestionably the most frequent and most tiresome discussion of adaptation." Nevertheless, Andrew summoned E. H. Gombrich and André Bazin as supporters for the argument that "one cannot dismiss adaptation since it is a fact of human practice":

We can and do correctly match items from different systems all the time: a tuba sound is more like a rock than a piece of string; it is more like a bear than a bird; more like a romanesque church than a baroque one. Adaptation would then become a matter of searching two systems of communication for elements of equivalent position in the system capable of eliciting a signified at a given level of pertinence, for example the description of a narrative action.[42]

Speculating about possibilities for future research in Film and Literature asks that we think about a question: What do we need to know? Elsewhere in his article, Andrew proposed that adaptation studies might continue fruitfully were Film and Literature brought "out of the realm of eternal principle and airy generalization, and onto the uneven but solid ground of artistic history, practice, and discourse" (14)—an indisputable suggestion but one that might simply foster more rigorous investigations of the transactions between classic literature and serious filmmaking. I think we more urgently need to know something else.

If in Gombrich's terms, knowledge about adaptation simply entails the ability to isolate systematic equivalences capable of generating the same signified, then the commercial media, never fussy about mixing forms, have long since beaten academics to the punch. Confronted by our century's distinctive feature—a media industry whose shared (and oppressive) representations converge from every side to structure even our unconscious lives—we have no idea how to fight back. Academic life and its resulting pedagogy are still bound to the word; the more supple tools that impinge upon us, images and sounds combined with language, we have not yet learned to use.

As a movement in the arts, sciences, and critical theory, postmodernism teaches that things repressed (objects, groups, signs, questions) return in displaced form. Ignored soup labels return as Warhol's avant-garde paintings, women's studies becomes feminist theory, and photographs of Vietnam appear on punk rock album covers. Similarly, Film and Literature, repressed as a topic by film studies' leading institutions and scholars, has for some time been reappearing as explorations into transactions between word and image. Prominent precedents for this position have long existed: Freud's positing of the unconscious (and the dream) as a rebus, Eisenstein's and Pound's fascination with the Chinese ideogram, Barthes's semiotic inquiries into the relationships between photograph and caption, Godard's experiments with language remotivating imagery, Eikhenbaum's thesis that filmwatching depends upon the viewer's accompanying images with his own "inner speech," Francis Yates's description of Renaissance memory systems founded on mentally stored images, Derrida's research into the vestigial hieroglyphic elements of our writing, and Alexandre Astruc's famous demand that we use the camera to *write*.[43] Why as students and teachers should we care about the relationship of word and image? Let me propose an answer, which I hope will provoke future work in a transformed field of Film and Literature.

In a provocative series of essays analyzing the decisive shift from orality to writing in ancient Greece, Eric A. Havelock demonstrated that every facet of a culture's life is influenced by its presiding means of communication.[44] Nearly fifty years ago, Arnold Hauser labeled the twentieth century "The Film Age."[45] Although film and television, and now computers, have steadily supplanted the book, we continue to live in a period of transition with the two forms, word and image, existing side by side. Commercial interests have long since learned *one* way of using the communications resources whose richness no other historical period can equal. The task facing all of us, especially Film and Literature scholars, involves rethinking the media's fait accompli, imagining new ways in which words and images can combine and new purposes for those combinations.

N O T E S

1. How a Film Theory Got Lost

1. Theodor Adorno, "Letter to Walter Benjamin," trans. Harry Zohn, in *Aesthetics and Politics*, ed. Fredric Jameson (London: Verso, 1938/1980), p. 129.

2. Thomas Schatz, *The Genius of the System: Hollywood Filmmaking in the Studio Era* (New York: Pantheon Books, 1988).

3. Peter Wollen, *Raiding the Icebox: Reflections on Twentieth-Century Culture* (Bloomington: Indiana University Press, 1993); Ray Batchelor, *Henry Ford: Mass Productions, Modernism, Design* (Manchester: Manchester University Press, 1994).

4. Noël Burch, *Life to Those Shadows* (Berkeley: University of California Press, 1990).

5. Colin MacCabe, *Godard: Image, Sounds, Politics* (Bloomington: Indiana University Press, 1980), p. 27.

6. Jean-Luc Godard, *Godard on Godard*, trans. Tom Milne (New York: Viking Press, 1972), p. 63.

7. Godard, *Godard on Godard*, p. 181.

8. Richard Abel, ed., *French Film Theory and Criticism*, vol. I: *1907–1921* (Princeton: Princeton University Press, 1988), pp. 138–139, 243, 315.

9. André Bazin, *What Is Cinema?* vol. 1, trans. Hugh Gray (Berkeley: University of California Press, 1967), p. 13.

10. Walter Benjamin, *One-Way Street*, trans. Edmund Jephcott and Kingsley Shorter (London: New Left Books, 1979), p. 255.

11. Paul Willemen, *Looks and Frictions: Essays in Cultural Studies and Film Theory* (Bloomington: Indiana University Press, 1994), p. 125.

12. Paul Hammond, ed., *The Shadow and Its Shadow: Surrealist Writings on the Cinema* (London: British Film Institute, 1978), p. 29.

13. Abel, *French Film Theory and Criticism*, vol. I, p. 242.

14. Willemen, *Looks and Frictions*, p. 131.

15. Hammond, *The Shadow and Its Shadow*, p. 29.

16. William Pietz, "The Problem of the Fetish, Part 1," *Res* 9 (1985).

17. Pietz, "The Problem of the Fetish," pp. 7–9.

18. Robert B. Ray, *The Avant-Garde Finds Andy Hardy* (Cambridge, Mass.: Harvard University Press, 1995).

19. Dudley Andrew, *André Bazin* (New York: Oxford University Press, 1978).

20. Bazin, *What Is Cinema?* vol. 2, trans. Hugh Gray (Berkeley: University of California Press, 1971).

21. Bazin, *What Is Cinema?* vol. 1, p. 21.

22. Bazin, *What Is Cinema?* vol. 1, p. 24.

23. Bazin, *What Is Cinema?* vol. 2, p. 60.

24. André Breton, *Manifestos of Surrealism*, trans. Richard Seaver and Helen R. Lane (Ann Arbor: University of Michigan Press, 1972), p. 26.

25. Max Ernst, *Beyond Painting and Other Writings by the Artist and His Friends* (New York: Wittenborn Schultz, 1948), p. 177.

26. Hammond, *The Shadow and Its Shadow*, p. 84.

27. Bazin, *What Is Cinema?* vol. 1, pp. 49–50.

28. See Friedrich A. Kittler, *Discourse Networks 1800/1900*, trans. Michael Metteer (Stanford: Stanford University Press, 1990).

29. Jim Hillier, ed., *Cahiers du Cinéma. The 1950s: Neo-Realism, Hollywood, New Wave* (Cambridge, Mass: Harvard University Press, 1985), p. 134.

30. Andrew Sarris, "Preminger's Two Periods: Studio and Solo," *Film Comment* 3, no. 3 (1965): p. 13.

31. Paul A. David, "Clio and the Economics of QWERTY," *American Economic Review* 75, no. 2 (1985); Peter Passell, "Why the Best Doesn't Always Win," *New York Times Magazine*, 5 May 1996, pp. 60–61.

32. Jonathan Rosenbaum, "The Films of Jean-Marie Straub and Danielle Huillet," in *Film at the Public: Programme for a Film Series* (New York: Public Theater, 1982).

33. Godard, *Godard on Godard*, pp. 64, 66.

34. Godard, *Godard on Godard*, p. 171.

35. Roland Barthes, "The Theory of the Text," trans. Geoff Bennington, in *Untying the Text: A Post-Structuralist Reader*, ed. Robert Young (Boston: Routledge & Kegan Paul, 1973/1981), p. 44.

36. Bill Nichols, ed., *Movies and Methods* (Berkeley: University of California Press, 1976), p. 76.

37. See Robert B. Ray, *A Certain Tendency of the Hollywood Cinema 1930–1980* (Princeton: Princeton University Press, 1985).

38. Abel, *French Film Theory and Criticism*, vol. I, p. 246.

39. Fredric Jameson and James Kavanagh, "The Weakest Link: Marxism in Literary Studies," in *The Left Academy II* (New York: Praeger, 1984), pp. 3–4.

40. Roland Barthes, *Image Music Text*, trans. Stephen Heath (New York: Hill and Wang, 1977), p. 166.

41. Barthes, *Roland Barthes*, trans. Richard Howard (New York: Hill and Wang, 1977), p. 71.

42. Ray, *The Avant-Garde Finds Andy Hardy*, pp. 10–12.

43. Gregory L. Ulmer, *Heuretics: The Logic of Invention* (Baltimore: Johns Hopkins University Press, 1994).

44. Marcel Jean, ed., *The Autobiography of Surrealism* (New York: Viking, 1980), 298–301; Hammond, *The Shadow and Its Shadow*, pp. 74–80.

45. Ray, *The Avant-Garde Finds Andy Hardy*, pp. 173–174.

2. Snapshots

1. Walter Benjamin, "N [Theoretics of Knowledge; Theory of Progress]," trans. Leigh Hafrey and Richard Sieburth, *The Philosophical Forum* 15, nos. 1–2 (1983–1984): p. 23.

2. Jean-Luc Godard, "Interview with Yvonne Baby," in *Breathless*, ed. Dudley Andrew (New Brunswick, N.J.: Rutgers University Press, 1987), p. 166.

3. Samuel Marx and Joyce Vandeveen, *Deadly Illusions: Jean Harlow and the Murder of Paul Bern* (New York: Random House, 1990), pp. 224–225.

4. See Noël Burch, "Film's Institutional Mode of Representation and the Soviet Response," *October* 11 (1979): pp. 77–96.

5. Benjamin, "N," p. 32.

6. Ian Jeffrey, *Photography: A Concise History* (New York: Oxford University Press, 1981), p. 240.

7. Dana Brand, "From the *Flâneur* to the Detective: Interpreting the City of Poe," in *Popular Fiction: Technology, Ideology, Production, Reading*, ed. Tony Bennett (London: Routledge, 1990), pp. 220–237.

8. Walter Benjamin, *Charles Baudelaire: A Lyric Poet in the Age of High Capitalism*, trans. Harry Zohn (London: New Left Books, 1973), p. 40.

9. Edgar Allan Poe, "The Man of the Crowd," in *The Portable Poe*, ed. Phillip Van Doren Stern (New York: Viking, 1945), p. 107. See Dana Brand's comment on this passage in "From the *Flâneur* to the Detective," pp. 220–221.

10. Poe, *The Portable Poe*, p. 118.

11. Roland Barthes, *S/Z*, trans. Richard Miller (New York: Hill and Wang, 1974), pp. 172–173.

12. Richard Sieburth, "Same Difference: The French *Physiologies*, 1840–1842," *Notebooks in Cultural Analysis*, no. 1 (1984): pp. 163, 167.

13. Benjamin, *Charles Baudelaire*, p. 39.

14. Daniel Goleman, "'Useful' Modes of Thinking Contribute to the Power of Prejudice," *New York Times*, 12 May 1987, C10.

15. Jeffrey, *Photography: A Concise History*, pp. 12–13.

16. Sieburth, "Same Difference: The French *Physiologies*," p. 184.

17. Poe, *The Portable Poe*, p. 112.

18. Paul Willemen, "Cinematic Discourse: The Problem of Inner Speech," *Screen* 22, no. 3 (1981): p. 78.

19. Edward Tenner, *Why Things Bite Back: Technology and the Revenge of Unintended Consequences* (New York: Alfred A. Knopf, 1996).

20. E. C. Bentley, *Trent's Last Case*, in *Three Famous Murder Novels*, ed. Bennett A. Cerf (New York: The Modern Library, 1945), p. 1.

21. Arthur Conan Doyle, *The Complete Sherlock Holmes* (Garden City, N.Y.: Doubleday, 1927), p. 467.

22. Susan Sontag, *On Photography* (New York: Farrar, Straus and Giroux, 1977), pp. 105–106.

23. James Lastra, "From the 'Captures Moment' to the Cinematic Image: Transformation in Pictorial Order," in *The Image in Dispute*, ed. Dudley Andrew (Austin: University of Texas Press, 1997), pp. 263–291; Arthur Conan Doyle, *The Unknown Conan Doyle: Essays on Photography*, ed. John Michael Gibson and Richard Lancelyn Green (London: Martin, Secker and Warburg, 1982).

24. Roland Barthes, "The Third Meaning: Research Notes on Several Eisenstein Stills," in *The Responsibility of Forms: Critical Essays on Music, Art, and Representation*, trans. Richard Howard (New York: Hill and Wang, 1985), pp. 41–62.

25. Roland Barthes, *Mythologies,* trans. Annette Lavers (New York: Hill and Wang, 1972), pp. 125, 127.

26. Willemen, "Cinematic Discourse," p. 64.

27. Quoted in *The Shadow and Its Shadow: Surrealist Writings on the Cinema,* ed. Paul Hammond (London: British Film Institute, 1978), pp. 42–43.

28. Barthes, "The Third Meaning," p. 59.

29. D. A. Miller, "Language of Detective Fiction: Fiction of Detective Language," in *The State of the Language,* ed. Leonard Michaels and Christopher Ricks (Berkeley: University of California Press, 1980), p. 482.

30. Roland Barthes, *Roland Barthes,* trans. Richard Howard (New York: Hill and Wang, 1977), pp. 54–55.

31. Roger Cardinal, "Pausing over Peripheral Detail," *Framework* [London] 30/31 (1986): p. 124.

32. Susan Sontag, *Against Interpretation* (New York: Delta, 1966), p. 14: "In place of a hermeneutics we need an erotics of art."

3. The Bordwell Regime and the Stakes of Knowledge

1. Cited by Hugh Honour, *Neo-Classicism* (New York: Penguin, 1977), p. 17.

2. Jean-François Lyotard, *The Postmodern Condition: A Report on Knowledge,* trans. Geoff Bennington and Brian Massumi (Minneapolis: University of Minnesota Press, 1984).

3. Auguste Comte, *Introduction to Positive Philosophy,* trans. Frederick Ferre (Indianapolis: Bobbs-Merrill, 1970), p. 2.

4. Ludwig Wittgenstein, *Tractatus Logico-Philosophicus,* trans. D. F. Pears and B. F. McGuiness (New York: Humanities Press, 1972), p. 151. This passage gives a fuller sense of the *Tractatus's* proximity to Comte: "The correct method would really be the following: to say nothing except what can be said, i.e., propositions of natural science—i.e., something that has nothing to do with philosophy—and then, whenever someone else wanted to say something metaphysical, to demonstrate to him that he had failed to give a meaning to certain signs in his propositions. Although it would not be satisfying to the other person—he would not have the feeling that we were teaching him philosophy—this method would be the only strictly correct one" (151).

5. Heinrich Wölfflin, *Principles of Art History,* trans. M. D. Hottinger (New York: Dover, 1932).

6. Cited in Heinrich Wölfflin, *Renaissance and Baroque,* trans. Kathrin Simon (Ithaca: Cornell University Press, 1966), p. 23.

7. Wölfflin, *Renaissance and Baroque,* p. 15.

8. Wölfflin, *Renaissance and Baroque,* p. 23.

9. T. F. Hoad, ed., *The Concise Oxford Dictionary of English Etymology* (Oxford: Oxford University Press, 1986), p. 34.

10. Wölfflin, *Principles of Art History,* pp. 14–15.

11. Arnold Hauser, *The Social History of Art,* vol. II, trans. Stanley Godman (New York: Vintage, 1951), pp. 173–174.

12. Roland Barthes, *Image Music Text,* trans. Stephen Heath (New York: Hill and Wang, 1977), p. 193.

13. On the baroque's refocusing, see Hauser, *The Social History of Art,* vol. II, p. 103: "Motifs which seem to be of only secondary significance for the real subject of the picture are often overbearingly prominent, whereas what is apparently the leading theme is devalued and suppressed." (Think of Derrida's *Spurs,* with its lengthy scrutiny of Nietzsche's apparently casual note, "I have forgotten my umbrella." Derrida, of course, frequently concentrates on the marginal and the frame.)

On the baroque's interdisciplinarity, see Honour's *Neo-Classicism* for a discussion of "composite art": "it was in the Rococo style that the intricate fusion of painting, sculpture and architecture reached its apogee" (20). (Think of poststructuralism's "composite" texts: e.g., *Roland Barthes, The Post Card*.)

14. In Patrick Waldberg, *Surrealism* (New York: Oxford University Press, 1965), p. 66.

15. Guillaume Apollinaire, "La Jolie Rousse," in *Selected Writings of Guillaume Apollinaire*, trans. Roger Shattuck (New York: New Directions, 1971), p. 195.

16. Sigmund Freud, *The Psychopathology of Everyday Life*, trans. Alan Tyson (New York: Norton, 1960), pp. 1–7.

17. Gregory Ulmer, "The Puncept in Grammatology," in *On Puns: The Foundation of Letters*, ed. Jonathan Culler (New York: Basil Blackwell, 1988), pp. 164–180.

18. Lyotard, *The Postmodern Condition*, p. xxv.

19. See Jacques Derrida, "Passe-Partout," in *The Truth in Painting*, trans. Geoff Bennington and Ian McLeod (Chicago: University of Chicago Press, 1987), pp. 1–13.

20. Lyotard, *The Postmodern Condition*, p. 41. Jonathan Culler has argued that the American academic reward system, with its demand for rapid and prolific publication, encourages interpretations of individual texts, an approach that "can generate an endless series of twenty-page articles" ("The Critical Assumption," *SCE Reports* 6 [Society for Critical Exchange] [Fall 1979]: pp. 77–85, 83).

21. David Bordwell, "Adventures in the Highlands of Theory," *Screen* 29, no. 1 (Winter 1988): pp. 95, 93.

22. David Bordwell, "Lowering the Stakes: Prospects for a Historical Poetics of Cinema," *Iris* 1, no. 1 (1983): p. 6.

23. Bordwell, "Adventures in the Highlands of Theory," p. 83.

24. David Bordwell, Janet Staiger, and Kristin Thompson, *The Classical Hollywood Cinema: Film Style and Mode of Production to 1960* (New York: Columbia University Press, 1985). Bordwell's other publications include several dozen articles; book-length studies of *The Passion of Joan of Arc*, Dreyer, Ozu, Eisenstein, and film narration; two textbooks co-authored with Thompson; a history of film style; and a history of film theory. Bordwell has denied that *CHC* is "the 'culmination' and 'central text' of what *Screen*'s reviewer called "the Wisconsin Project" ("Adventures in the Highlands of Theory," p. 79). The book, however, received extravagant praise from its reviewers: see note 32.

25. Michel de Certeau, *Heterologies: Discourse on the Other*, trans. Brian Massumi (Minneapolis: University of Minnesota Press, 1986), pp. 212–213.

26. "Not that [historiography] speaks the truth; never has the historian pretended to do that. Rather, with his apparatus for the critical reading of documents, the scholar effaces error from the 'fables' of the past. The territory that he occupies is acquired through a diagnosis of the false. He hollows out a place for his discipline in the terrain of received tradition. . . . [H]e spends his time pursuing the false, rather than in the construction of the true, as though truth could be produced only by means of determining error" (Certeau, *Heterologies*, pp. 200–201).

27. David Bordwell and Kristin Thompson, "Linearity, Materialism, and the Study of Early Cinema," *Wide Angle* 5, no. 3 (1983): pp. 4–15. This article cites all of the important Burch articles.

28. Roland Barthes, "From Science to Literature," in *The Rustle of Language*, trans. Richard Howard (New York: Hill and Wang, 1986): pp. 7–8.

29. Lyotard, *The Postmodern Condition*, p. 16. In his last interview, Foucault termed the polemical mode "sterilizing," asking, "Has anyone ever seen a new idea come out of a polemic? And how could it be otherwise, given that here the interlocutors are in-

cited, not to advance, not to take more and more risks in what they say, but to fall back continually on the rights that they claim on their legitimacy, which they must defend, and on the affirmation of their innocence" ("Polemics, Politics, and Problematizations: An Interview," in *The Foucault Reader,* ed. Paul Rabinow [New York: Pantheon, 1984], p. 383).

30. I should say that I do not object to Bordwell's advertising BST's work. Indeed, I thought enough of this tactic to try it myself in this essay's opening: I am a member of the Vulgar Boatmen.

31. I do not find this statement incompatible with my earlier analogy, classicism: normal science:: the baroque: revolutionary science. Should revolutionary science become the norm, a program calling for a moratorium on new ideas for the sake of developing a few existing ones might seem radical. Bordwell, in fact, argues that precisely this situation has come about in film studies (see "Lowering the Stakes"), implying that his own more restricted research program provides a radical alternative to film studies' unchecked theorizing (see "Adventures in the Highlands of Theory," especially p. 85). The issue, of course, concerns the extent to which merely fifteen years of what Bordwell calls "SLAB Theory" (Saussure, Lacan, Althusser, and Barthes) (97) constitutes so complete a replacement of the previous classicism that his own revision is made "radical." If nothing else, Bordwell's claim suggests how "radical" remains an attractive label within American culture. The movie *Red Dawn* (1984) even created a situation in which Americans get to become guerrillas, just like Che Guevara and Fidel Castro.

32. The first quotation comes from Tom Gunning, *Wide Angle* 7, no. 3 (1985): p. 74; the second from Robert C. Allen, blurb on the back cover of another Columbia University Press book, Robin Wood's *Hollywood from Vietnam to Reagan* (1986). Even taking into account the form's requisite hyperbole, the Allen comment seems significantly formulated.

33. See Thomas Kuhn, *The Structure of Scientific Revolutions* (Chicago: University of Chicago Press, 1970), p. 20. By contrast, Michel de Certeau noted that Foucault's histories seemed to originate in "bouts of surprise . . . which have been, from Aristotle to Wittgenstein, the inaugurators of philosophical activity. Something that exceeds the thinkable and opens the possibility of 'thinking otherwise' bursts in through comical, incongruous, or paradoxical half-openings of discourse" (*Heterologies,* 194).

In fairness to BST, I would point out that while a resumé of *CHC* makes the book seem predictable, its impressive power results from the evidentiary weight sustaining every argument. Perhaps we need to remind ourselves that such a systematic working out of ideas should not be gainsaid. Having spent a brief two paragraphs summarizing Kuhn's arguments, David A. Hollinger wisely observed that "once this sense of historical development is abstracted from *The Structure of Scientific Revolutions* it sounds like a set of truisms. This fact only serves to illustrate a point Kuhn has insisted upon: concrete examples, like Kuhn's achievement in the history of science, have a staying power distinct from that of the general principles they embody. Had Kuhn written the foregoing two paragraphs instead of having written *The Structure of Scientific Revolutions,* it is doubtful that he would have inspired so many attempts to 'apply Kuhn's ideas to history'" ("T. S. Kuhn's Theory of Science and Its Implications for History," in *Paradigms and Revolutions: Applications and Appraisals of Thomas Kuhn's Philosophy of Science,* ed. Gary Gutting [Notre Dame, Ind.: University of Notre Dame Press, 1980], p. 199).

On the other hand, I will suggest later in this essay that even very brief propositions, if formulated strikingly, can inspire an enormous body of subsequent work: e.g., Lacan's "The unconscious is structured like a language." See, too, this paragraph from Nietzsche's *Gay Science,* which Barthes and Foucault often seemed merely to be annotating: "*Something for the industrious*. . . . So far, everything that has given color to existence still lacks a history: or, where could one find a history of love, of avarice, of envy, of conscience, of pity, or of cruelty? Even a comparative history of law, or merely of punishment, is completely lacking so far. Has anyone yet conducted research into the different ways of dividing the day and the consequences of a regular arrangement of work, holiday, and rest? Does one know the moral effects of food? . . . Have the experiences of living together been assembled: for example, the experiences in the monasteries? Has the dialectic of marriage and friendship been presented as yet?" (*The Portable Nietzsche*, ed. Walter Kaufmann [New York: Viking Press, 1968], p. 90).

34. Foucault, *The Foucault Reader*, p. 74.

35. Bertolt Brecht, *Brecht on Theatre*, trans. John Willett (New York: Hill and Wang, 1964), pp. 34–35.

36. Lyotard, *The Postmodern Condition*, p. 24. This passage raises an issue critical to knowledge's institutional development, one repeatedly dramatized by psychoanalysis's traumatic history: what is teaching's goal, the invitation to disciples or the incitement to heresy?

37. Nietzsche, *The Gay Science* § pp. 344, 28–283 (*"How we, too, are still pious"*).

38. Roland Barthes, "Michelet Today," in *The Rustle of Language*, pp. 198–199, 203.

39. Kuhn, *The Structure of Scientific Revolutions*, pp. 75–76.

40. David Bordwell, *The Films of Carl-Theodor Dreyer* (Berkeley: University of California Press, 1981), pp. 93–116.

41. Bordwell, Staiger, and Thompson, *CHC*, pp. 3–84.

42. See Foucault's "What Is an Author?" in *The Foucault Reader*, pp. 101–120.

43. Foucault, "Truth and Power," in *The Foucault Reader*, pp. 8–71.

44. See note 22.

45. Bordwell, "Adventures in the Highlands of Theory," p. 89.

46. Jean-Luc Godard, *Jean-Luc Godard: A Critical Anthology*, ed. Toby Mussman (New York: Dutton, 1968), p. 103. This interview originally appeared in *Cahiers du Cinéma* (December 1962).

47. Frederick Crews, *Skeptical Engagements* (New York: Oxford University Press, 1986), pp. 159–178.

48. Bordwell and Thompson, "Linearity, Materialism, and the Study of Early Cinema," p. 7.

49. See John Hess, "La Politique des auteurs," *Jump Cut* 1 (May–June 1974): 19–22; and *Jump Cut* 2 (July–August 1974): pp. 20–22.

50. Foucault, "Truth and Power," in *The Foucault Reader*, p. 74. While Bordwell has not criticized his method's epistemology, he has sought to democratize it. He administers the University of Wisconsin's Film Scholars Fellowship Program, which provides funds for researchers to study for a semester in the university's unmatched archives. In arranging for this program, Bordwell has indeed made the film studies apparatus a better one.

51. Thomas Kuhn, "The Essential Tension: Tradition and Innovation in Scientific Research," in *The Essential Tension* (Chicago: University of Chicago Press, 1977), pp. 225–239.

52. For a discussion of the uneven, "undemocratic" nature of scientific achievement and its disproportionate concentration in a small group of advanced researchers, see Derek J. De Solla Price, *Little Science, Big Science* (New York: Columbia University Press, 1963).

53. The leading discussion of this point is Gregory L. Ulmer's *Applied Grammatology: Post(e)-Pedagogy from Jacques Derrida to Joseph Beuys* (Baltimore: Johns Hopkins University Press, 1985).

54. See Warren F. Motte, Jr., ed., *Oulipo: A Primer of Potential Literature* (Lincoln: University of Nebraska Press, 1986).

55. Paul Feyerabend, *Against Method* (London: New Left Books, 1975), p. 20.

56. See "La taylorisation de la recherche," in *(Auto)critique de la science,* ed. A. Jaubert and J.-M. Lévy-Leblond (Paris: Seuil, 1973), pp. 291–293. Cited in Lyotard, *The Postmodern Condition,* p. 95, footnote 131.

57. Paul Feyerabend, *Science in a Free Society* (London: New Left Books, 1978), pp. 88–89.

58. Feyerabend, *Against Method,* p. 32.

59. Roger Shattuck, *The Innocent Eye* (New York: Farrar, Straus and Giroux, 1984), pp. 184–185.

60. Lyotard, *The Postmodern Condition,* p. 17 (emphasis added).

61. Feyerabend, *Against Method,* p. 19, note 7.

62. Walter Benjamin, "One-Way Street," in *Reflections,* trans. Edmund Jephcott (New York: Harvest/HBJ, 1978), p. 65.

63. "What liberates metaphor, symbol, emblem from poetic *mania,* what manifests its power of subversion, is the *preposterous,* that 'bewilderment' which Fourier was so good at getting into his examples, to the scorn of any rhetorical respectability. . . . The logical future of metaphor would therefore be the gag" (Roland Barthes, *Roland Barthes,* trans. Richard Howard [New York: Hill and Wang, 1977], p. 81). For the relationship between knowledge production and practical jokes, see *Re/Search # 11: Pranks* (San Francisco: Re/Search Publications, 1987).

64. Gregory L. Ulmer, *Teletheory: Grammatology in the Age of Video* (New York: Routledge, 1989).

65. Barthes, *Roland Barthes,* p. 131.

66. Feyerabend, *Against Method,* pp. 25–26.

67. Richard Boyd, "Metaphor and Theory Change: What Is 'Metaphor' a Metaphor For?" in *Metaphor and Thought,* ed. Andrew Ortony (Cambridge: Cambridge University Press, 1979), pp. 359–360, 363.

68. Bordwell, "Adventures in the Highlands of Theory," pp. 95–96.

69. See Shoshana Felman, "Psychoanalysis and Education: Teaching Terminable and Interminable," in her *Jacques Lacan and the Adventure of Insight* (Cambridge, Mass.: Harvard University Press, 1987), pp. 69–97.

70. Dan Sperber, *Rethinking Symbolism,* trans. Alice L. Morton (Cambridge: Cambridge University Press, 1975), p. 101. In suggesting that metaphors function as "memory images" to store important information, George A. Miller points out that "the vagueness of the image is critical to its utility. If memory images had to be completely detailed, like photographs, they could not preserve the incomplete information given by written descriptions" ("Images and Models, Similes and Metaphors," in *Metaphor and Thought,* p. 205).

71. For me, Burch's terms have proved the most stimulating: "the diegetic effect," "the illusionist rapture," "illegibility" (of an image's information), "pillow shots" (nonnarrative transitional moments in Ozu's films), "acentric images" (in Porter's "primitive" cinema).

72. Perhaps the leading essay is Brian Henderson's "Toward a Non-Bourgeois Camera Style," in *Movies and Methods,* ed. Bill Nichols (Berkeley: University of California Press, 1976), 422–438. Most of Nöel Burch's postformalist work seems also to issue from Godard's remark.

73. Walter Benjamin, "Some Reflections on Kafka," in *Illuminations,* trans. Harry Zohn (New York: Schocken, 1969), p. 144.

74. For *"mots-valeurs,"* see "Outcomes of the Text," in *The Rustle of Language,*

pp. 247–249, and *Roland Barthes*, pp. 127, 129. For "fashion words," "mana-words," and "color-words," see *Roland Barthes*, pp. 127, 129.

75. Foucault, "What Is an Author?" in *The Foucault Reader*, p. 114.

76. When I speak of Marx or Freud as founders of discursivity, I mean that they made possible not only a certain number of analogies but also (and equally important) a certain number of differences. They have created a possibility for something other than their discourse, yet something belonging to what they founded. To say that Freud founded psychoanalysis does not (simply) mean that we find the concept of the libido or the technique of dream analysis in the works of Karl Abraham or Melanie Klein; it means that Freud made possible a certain number of divergences—with respect to his own texts, concepts, and hypotheses—that all arise from the psychoanalytic discourse itself. See Foucault, *The Foucault Reader*, pp. 114–115.

77. Roland Barthes, "Inaugural Lecture, Collège de France," in *A Barthes Reader*, ed. Susan Sontag (New York: Hill and Wang, 1982), p. 465.

78. See Benjamin's *Charles Baudelaire: A Lyric Poet in the Era of High Capitalism*, trans. Harry Zohn (London: Verso, 1983). Benjamin originally planned his *Arcades Project* as a collage history of nineteenth-century Paris. For a leading discussion of collage and its relationship to film and photography, see Gregory L. Ulmer, "The Object of Post-Criticism," in *The Anti-Aesthetic: Essays on Postmodern Culture*, ed. Hal Foster (Port Townsend, Wash.: Bay Press, 1983), pp. 83–110.

In a very suggestive remark, Arnold Hauser observes that "the artistic outlook of the baroque is, in a word, cinematic; the incidents represented seem to have been overheard and spied out; every indication that might betray consideration for the beholder is blotted out, everything is presented in apparent accordance with pure chance" (*The Social History of Art*, vol. II, p. 176).

79. See Gilles Deleuze, "Nomad Thought," in *The New Nietzsche*, ed. David B. Allison (New York: Delta, 1977), pp. 142–149.

80. Having taught contemporary theory for the past few years, I have noted another significant advantage of normal science: it serves as the *doxical* background (often provided in traditional literature courses) against which both students and teacher take great pleasure in revolting. Indeed, the engine of desire on which contemporary criticism classrooms generally run involves the pleasure of perversion, which, as Barthes saw, "is always underestimated" (*Roland Barthes*, p. 63). (It is, perhaps, the pleasure I derive from writing this essay, from staking out an elsewhere for film studies.) Of course, this pleasure, too (especially?), can grow stale: what would a field be like in which the revolutionary mode became normal science? We do not yet know, though Bordwell has thought about this question: see note 31.

81. Roland Barthes, *Criticism and Truth* (Minneapolis: University of Minnesota Press, 1987), p. 66. The original French version appeared in 1966. For another discussion of "the crisis in commentary," see my "Response to Leland Poague's 'All I Can See Is the Flags': *Fort Apache* and the Visibility of History," *Cinema Journal* 27, no. 3 (Spring 1988): pp. 45–49.

82. "*Mannerism.* . . . It is typified by stylistic trickery and a liking for bizarre effects. . . . Mannerist art conveys a sense of neurotic disquiet, and tends to concentrate on style rather than content, while the content itself is often complicated and esoteric. In the Decorative Arts there is a taste for virtuosity and the unexpected" (Edward Lucie-Smith, *The Thames and Hudson Dictionary of Art Terms* [New York: Thames and Hudson, 1984], p. 116).

83. See, for example, the Frederick Crews article cited in note 47, and René Wellek, "Destroying Literary Studies," in *The New Criterion Reader*, ed. Hilton Kramer (New York: The Free Press, 1988), pp. 29–36.

84. Richard Rorty, *Philosophy and the Minor of Nature* (Princeton: Princeton University Press, 1979). See also Rorty's "Philosophy as a Kind of Writing: An Essay on Derrida," in his *Consequences of Pragmatism* (Minneapolis: University of Minnesota, 1982), pp. 90–109. In this latter essay, Rorty, while sympathetic to the baroque tradition, underestimates its capacity to be other than a mere deconstructive gadfly, preying on the solemnity of classicism.

85. Ulmer, *Applied Grammatology*, p. 300.

86. Perhaps the most telling formulation of this modern discontent is Flaubert's: "As for combating [an obviously ignorant opinion], why not combat the contrary, which is quite as stupid as it is? There are a whole crowd of such topics which annoy me just as much whatever way they are approached. . . . Thus Voltaire, mesmerism, Napoleon, the French Revolution, Catholicism, etc. Whether one speaks good or ill of them I am equally irritated" (cited in Jonathan Culler, *Flaubert: The Uses of Uncertainty* [Ithaca: Cornell University Press, 1974], p. 167).

87. For a suggestive use of puns and homonyms applied to the vital issue of nuclear war, see Derrida's "No Apocalypse, Not Now (full speed ahead, seven missiles, seven missives)," *Diacritics* (Summer 1984): pp. 20–31.

88. For a discussion of Surrealism's practical applications, see Gregory L. Ulmer, "Textshop for Psychoanalysis: On De-programming Freshmen Platonists," *College English* 49, no. 7 (November 1987): pp. 756–769. Barthes's research strategy, which repudiated normal science's single-mindedness for a collaborative (Barthes worked in seminars) drifting, seems the intellectual equivalent of the Situationists' *dérive*, a strategy for urban planning itself extrapolated from Surrealist automatic writing. See Guy Debord, "Theory of the *Dérive*," in *Situationist International Anthology*, ed. Ken Knabb (Berkeley: Bureau of Public Secrets, 1981) pp. 50–54.

89. Jonathan Culler, "At the Boundaries: Barthes and Derrida," in *Proceedings of the Northeastern University Center for Literary Studies*, vol. 1 (1983): p. 28.

90. "[T]he new semiology—or the new mythology— . . . it too has become in some sort mythical: any student can and does denounce the bourgeois or petit-bourgeois character of such and such a form (of life, of thought, of consumption). In other words, a mythological doxa has been created: denunciation, demystification (or demythification), has itself become discourse, stock of phrases, catechistic declaration . . . " ("Change the Object Itself: Mythology Today" [1971], in *Image Music Text*, p. 166).

91. For a discussion of professionalization's effect on English departments and their increased susceptibility to fashionable theories, see Brian McCrea, *Addison and Steele Are Dead: The English Department, Its Canon, and the Professionalization of Literary Criticism* (Newark: University of Delaware Press, 1989).

92. Walter Benjamin, *The Origin of German Tragic Drama*, trans. John Osborne (London: New Left Books, 1977), p. 175.

93. Laura Mulvey and Jon Halliday, eds., *Douglas Sirk* (Edinburgh: Edinburgh Film Festival, 1972); *Sirk on Sirk* (New York: Viking Press, 1972).

94. James Harvey, "Sirkumstantial Evidence," *Film Comment* (July–August 1978): p. 54.

95. See Paul Willemen, "Distanciation and Douglas Sirk," in *Douglas Sirk*, pp. 23–29; and Willemen, "Towards an Analysis of the Sirkian System," in *Douglas Sirk*, pp. 11–17.

96. Harvey, "Sirkumstantial Evidence," p. 54.

97. See Brecht, "The Popular and the Realistic," in *Brecht on Brecht*, pp. 109–110; and Sylvia Harvey, "Whose Brecht? Memories for the Eighties," *Screen* 23, no. 1 (May–June 1982): pp. 45–59.

98. Susan Sontag "Notes on 'Camp,'" in *Against Interpretation* (New York: Delta, 1966), p. 277.

99. See also Benjamin's remark "The devaluation of the world of objects in allegory is outdone within the world of objects itself by the commodity" in "Central Park," *New German Critique* 34 (Winter 1985): p. 34.

100. Quoted in Sylvia Harvey, *May '68 and Film Culture* (London: British Film Institute, 1978), p. 115.

101. See Annette Kuhn, *Women's Pictures: Feminism and the Cinema* (London: Routledge and Kegan Paul, 1982), pp. 3–18, pp. 156–196.

102. On "encrustations," see Tony Bennett, "Text and Social Process: The Case of James Bond," *Screen Education* 41 (Winter/Spring 1982): p. 314.

103. See *Screen* 17, no. 4 (Winter 1976–1977): pp. 121–124, for Jonathan Rosenbaum's critique and Bordwell and Thompson's reply.

104. Roland Barthes, "To the Seminar," in *The Rustle of Language*, p. 338.

4. Tracking

1. The term "AABA song" refers to the Tin Pan Alley norm of chorus/chorus/bridge/chorus. Show tunes typically began with a "verse," an introductory section that occurred only once. While maintaining the AABA form, rock and roll dropped the verse, except in such rare cases as the Lennon-McCartney "Do You Want to Know a Secret?" with its opening "You'll never know how much I really love you / You'll never know how much I really care." This move, and the inclusion of Broadway's "Till There Was You" on their first American LP, suggest how much the Lennon-McCartney team owed to Tin Pan Alley.

2. Quoted in Stephen Holden's "Paul Simon's Journey to Brazil and Beyond," *New York Times*, 14 October 1990.

3. Public Enemy's Hank Shocklee, quoted in "Ebony and Ivory," an interview/conversation between Paul Simon and Hank Shocklee, *Spin*, January 1991, p. 84.

4. Mark Dery, "Public Enemy: Confrontation," *Keyboard*, September 1990, p. 84: "Rap, by definition, is political music. Fabricated from stolen snatches of prerecorded music by smash-and-grab producers who frequently thumb their noses at copyright laws, it is the musical equivalent of shoplifting." Despite this remark, Dery's article displays considerable sympathy for rap in general and Shocklee in particular.

5. See Walter Benjamin, "Eduard Fuchs, Collector and Historian," in *One-Way Street and Other Writings*, trans. Edmund Jephcott and Kingsley Shorter (London: New Left Books, 1979), pp. 349–386.

6. Susan Buck-Morss, *The Dialectics of Seeing: Walter Benjamin and the Arcades Project* (Cambridge, Mass.: MIT Press, 1989), p. 241.

7. Quoted by Buck-Morss, *The Dialectics of Seeing*, pp. 240–241; emphasis mine.

8. "The more probable (banal) the message, the less information it conveys" (Gregory L. Ulmer, *Applied Grammatology* [Baltimore: Johns Hopkins University Press, 1985], p. 308).

9. Meaghan Morris puts the matter bluntly: "I get the feeling that somewhere in some English publisher's vault there is a master disk from which thousands of versions of the same article . . . are being run off under different names with minor variations" ("Banality in Cultural Studies," in *Logics of Television: Essays in Cultural Criticism*, ed. Patricia Mellencamp [Bloomington: Indiana University Press, 1990], p. 21).

While the *Wall Street Journal* has denounced this tendency as indicative of American academics' overwhelming leftism (see "Politically Correct," *Wall Street Journal*, 26 November 1990), it in fact signals precisely the opposite: a commitment to capitalism and business-as-usual. Since at least the eighteenth century, ideas (like any product) have been subject to commodification. But what marks contemporary intellectual life is the intense speed with which even the most critical positions can become the newest way to make a living. With the chronic oversupply of Ph.D.'s enabling the humblest colleges to link promotion, tenure, and now hiring itself to publication, more and more people are producing more and more books and articles. Because these people are often working on deadlines (at my university, assistant professors have only five years before the tenure decision), they inevitably gravitate to hot areas, those methodologies and topics that ensure publication. As a result, cultural criticism, more than ever before, is now subject to the boom-and-bust cycles that have always haunted capitalism.

This development has real effects: at any given moment, everyone seems to be writing about the same thing—and then, no one is. Morris cites a Japanese media analyst's coolness toward a collection containing several essays on Foucault: "Ah Foucault . . . I'm very sorry, but there's no boom" ("Banality in Cultural Studies," *Discourse* 10 [Spring–Summer 1988]: p. 5.) (This essay is a slightly different version of the one cited above.) Again the pop analogy seems appropriate: a hit parade of critical ideas that changes every month.

10. See Walter Ong's *Orality and Literacy* (London: Methuen, 1982) for a summary of research on this topic. Jack Goody's books are more specific but equally interesting. See especially *The Domestication of the Savage Mind* (Cambridge: Cambridge University Press, 1977) and *The Logic of Writing and the Organization of Society* (Cambridge: Cambridge University Press, 1986).

11. Ong, *Orality and Literacy*, p. 51.

12. The pioneer in extending this argument to music was Glenn Gould. In his famous 1966 essay "The Prospects of Recording," Gould stated flatly that "we must be prepared to accept the fact that, for better or worse, recording will forever alter our notions about what is appropriate to the performance of music" (*The Glenn Gould Reader*, ed. Tim Page [New York: Knopf, 1984], p. 337). In particular, Gould maintained that the advent of tape splicing, by means of which perfect performances could be constructed in the studio, created for live performances audience expectations impossible to satisfy. In this context, classical performances became what Gould called "the last blood sport," something like a high-wire act where the audience waits breathlessly for the fall.

Significantly, Gould argued that this development cuts both ways. On one hand, it encourages conservatism among performers, afraid to take on new or difficult pieces for audiences grown unaccustomed to, and ultimately intolerant of, mistakes of any kind. On the other hand, recordings create active listeners who themselves could, by taking charge of their own editing, develop utterly nonconformist attitudes toward music and its history. If rap recording seems the result of this latter development, the spread of lip-syncing and tapes in "live" performance appears to issue from the former. All discussions about contemporary music and its technology should begin with Gould's warning that "the technology of electronic forms makes it highly improbable that we will move in any direction but one of even greater intensity and complexity" (*The Glenn Gould Reader*, p. 352).

13. Glenn Gould was quick to spot the obvious analogy between the recording process and filmmaking: "one should be free to 'shoot' a Beethoven sonata or a Bach fugue in or out of sequence, intercut almost without restriction, apply postproduction techniques as required, and . . . the composer, the performer, and above all the listener will be better served thereby" (*The Glenn Gould Reader*, p. 359).

14. Guy Debord, *The Society of the Spectacle* (Detroit: Black and Red, 1977), sec. 1.

15. In his interesting book *The Recording Angel: Explorations in Phonography* (New York: McGraw Hill, 1987), Evan Eisenberg proposes that "records and radio were

the proximate cause of the Jazz Age. . . . [R]ecords not only disseminated jazz, but in-seminated it—. . . . [I]n some ways they created what we call jazz" (143–144). To avoid paying royalties, groups such as King Oliver's Creole Jazz Band and Armstrong's Hot Five replaced published songs with on-the-spot improvisations whose recording granted them a permanence they would otherwise never have had.

16. Jacques Derrida, "Plato's Pharmacy," in *Dissemination,* trans. Barbara Johnson (Chicago: University of Chicago Press, 1981), pp. 61–171.

17. Public Enemy's Hank Shocklee has made explicit the implications of sampling and sequencing:

We don't like musicians. We don't *respect* musicians. . . . In dealing with rap, you have to be innocent and ignorant of music. Trained musicians are not ignorant of music, and they cannot be innocent to it. They understand it, and that's what keeps them from dealing with things out of the ordinary. . . . [Public Enemy is] a musician's *nightmare.* (*Keyboard,* September 1990, pp. 82–83)

Another Shocklee remark indicates what's at stake: "You get a person who says, 'I don't have time to study an instrument.' Rappers sample" (*Spin,* January 1991, p. 61).

18. Marianna Torgovnick, "Experimental Critical Writing," *Profession* 90 (1990): pp. 25–27.

19. Gregory L. Ulmer, *Teletheory: Grammatology in the Age of Video* (New York: Routledge, 1989), pp. 18–19.

20. For a preliminary report on this project, see my *Avant-Garde Finds Andy Hardy* (Cambridge, Mass.: Harvard University Press, 1995).

5. How to Start an Avant-Garde

1. Jerrold Seigel, *Bohemian Paris: Culture, Politics, and the Boundaries of Bourgeois Life, 1830–1930* (New York: Viking, 1986), p. 295.

2. Gertrude Stein, "Composition as Explanation," in *Selected Writings of Gertrude Stein,* ed. Carl Van Vechten (New York: The Modern Library, 1962), pp. 514–515.

3. Francis Haskell's "Enemies of Modern Art," in his *Past and Present in Art and Taste* (New Haven: Yale University Press, 1987), pp. 207–221, is the most important discussion of my topic and one to which I am greatly indebted. Charles Rosen's and Henri Zerner's brilliant essay, "The Ideology of the Licked Surface: Official Art," appears in their *Romanticism and Realism: The Mythology of Nineteenth-Century Art* (New York: Viking, 1984), pp. 203–232.

4. Harrison C. White and Cynthia A. White, *Canvases and Careers: Institutional Change in the French Painting World* (Chicago: University of Chicago Press, 1993).

5. Andy Warhol, *The Philosophy of Andy Warhol* (New York: Harvest/HBJ, 1975), p. 92.

6. Quoted in Jerry Hopkins, *Elvis: A Biography* (New York: Simon and Schuster, 1971), p. 136.

7. Quoted in F. W. J. Hemmings, *Culture and Society in France, 1848–1898* (New York: Scribner's, 1971), p.177. This famous passage, in a slightly different translation, also appears in Haskell, "Enemies of Modern Art," pp. 209–210 and Seigel, *Bohemian Paris,* p. 308.

8. Seigel, *Bohemian Paris,* p. 297.

6. How to Teach Cultural Studies

1. François Truffaut, "A Certain Tendency of the French Cinema," in *Movies and Methods,* ed. Bill Nichols (Berkeley: University of California Press, 1976), p. 231.

2. Truffaut, "A Certain Tendency of the French Cinema," p. 237, note 9.

3. Wheeler Winston Dixon, *The Early Film Criticism of François Truffaut* (Bloomington: Indiana University Press, 1993), p. 79.

4. Dixon, *The Early Film Criticism of François Truffaut*, p. 87.

5. W. J. Bate, *Criticism: The Major Texts* (New York: Harcourt Brace Jovanovich, 1970), p. 350.

6. Anton Kaes, Martin Jay, and Edward Dimendberg, eds., *The Weimar Republic Sourcebook* (Berkeley: University of California Press, 1994), p. 131.

7. Walter Benjamin, *Reflections*, trans. Edmund Jephcott (New York: Harvest/HBJ, 1978), p. 221.

8. Bertolt Brecht, *Brecht on Theatre*, trans. John Willet (New York: Hill and Wang, 1964), p. 180.

9. Robert Gibson, ed., *Modern French Poets on Poetry* (Cambridge: Cambridge University Press, 1979), p. 150.

10. Jim Hillier, ed., *Cahiers du Cinéma. The 1950s: Neo-Realism, Hollywood, New Wave* (Cambridge, Mass: Harvard University Press, 1985), p. 9.

11. André Bazin, *What Is Cinema?* vol. 1, trans. Hugh Gray (Berkeley: University of California Press, 1967), pp. 21–52.

12. Gregory L. Ulmer, *Heuretics: The Logic of Invention* (Baltimore: Johns Hopkins University Press, 1994), pp. 8–11.

13. André Breton, *Manifestoes of Surrealism*, trans. Richard Seaver and Helen R. Lane (Ann Arbor: University of Michigan Press, 1972).

14. Susan Sontag, *On Photography* (New York: Farrar, Straus and Giroux, 1977), pp. 4, 22.

15. Bertolt Brecht, *The Messingkauf Dialogues*, trans. John Willet (London: Methuen, 1965), pp. 15–16.

16. Peter Graham, *The New Wave* (Garden City, N.Y.: Doubleday, 1968), pp. 17–23.

17. Jean-Luc Godard, *Godard on Godard*, trans. Tom Milne (New York: Viking, 1972), pp. 171–196.

18. Truffaut, "A Certain Tendency of the French Cinema," p. 230.

19. *Cahiers du Cinéma. The 1950s*, p. 22.

20. Charles Rosen and Henri Zerner, *Romanticism and Realism: The Mythology of Nineteenth-Century Art* (New York: Viking, 1984), pp. 203–232.

21. Godard, *Godard on Godard*, p. 171.

22. Godard, *Godard on Godard*, p. 181.

23. Sherry Turkle, "Dynasty," *London Review of Books* (December 1990): p. 8.

24. Jean-Paul Sartre, "Existentialism Is a Humanism," in *Existentialism from Dostoevsky to Sartre*, ed. Walter Kaufmann (New York: New American Library, 1975), p. 287.

25. Godard, *Godard on Godard*, p. 76.

26. Sartre, "Existentialism Is a Humanism," p. 305.

27. Godard, *Godard on Godard*, p. 60.

28. Sartre, "Existentialism Is a Humanism," pp. 296, 297–298.

29. Godard, *Godard on Godard*, p. 223.

30. Jean-Paul Sartre, *Nausea*, trans. Lloyd Alexander (New York: New Directions, 1964), p. 39.

31. Godard, *Godard on Godard*, p. 221.

32. Paul Hammond, ed., *The Shadow and Its Shadow: Surrealist Writings on the Cinema* (London: British Film Institute, 1978), p. 19.

33. Hammond, *The Shadow and Its Shadow*, pp. 42–43.

34. Roland Barthes, *Roland Barthes*, trans. Richard Howard (New York: Hill and Wang, 1977), p. 117.

35. *Cahiers du Cinéma. The 1950s*, p. 116.

36. Walter Benjamin, *Understanding Brecht*, trans. Anna Bostock (London: New Left Books, 1977), pp. 106–107.

37. Jean-Luc Comolli and Jean Narboni, "Cinema/Ideology/Criticism," in *Movies and Methods*, p. 27.

38. Dixon, *The Early Film Criticism of François Truffaut*, pp. 154, 73.

39. Zdenek Felix and Martin Schwander, *Cindy Sherman: Photographic Work 1975–1995* (New York: Schirmer, 1995), p. 11.

40. Frank Lentricchia, "Last Will and Testament of an Ex-Literary Critic," *Lingua Franca*, September/October 1996; Jane Tompkins, *A Life in School: What the Teacher Learned* (New York: Addison-Wesley, 1996).

7. The Mystery of Edward Hopper

1. See Gail Levin, *Edward Hopper: The Art and the Artist*, exhibition catalogue (New York: Whitney Museum of Art, 1980), p. 58.

2. Walter Ong, *Orality and Literacy: The Technologizing of the Word* (New York: Routledge, 1982). See also the work of Gregory L. Ulmer: *Applied Grammatology: Post(e)-Pedagogy from Jacques Derrida to Joseph Beuys* (Baltimore: Johns Hopkins University Press, 1984) and *Teletheory: Grammatology in the Age of Video* (New York: Routledge, 1989).

3. As an example of oral logic, Ong (*Orality and Literacy*, p. 51) describes a scene from R. Luria's famous study *Cognitive Development: Its Cultural and Social Foundation*. Asked to identify the one dissimilar object in a group consisting of a hammer, saw, log, and hatchet, illiterate subjects, accustomed more to concrete, situational thinking than to such abstractions as "tool," insist upon the relatedness of all four. "They're all alike," one responded. "The saw will saw the log and the hatchet will chop it into small pieces. If one of these has to go, I'd throw out the hatchet. It doesn't do as good a job as a saw." When presented with the "correct" notion involving the concept of "tool," the same man stuck to his guns: "YES, but even if we have tools, we still need wood—otherwise we can't build anything." While this answer would get you nowhere on an SAT test (an exam based almost entirely on the methods of literate culture), it does amount to a kind of thinking. Although we take for granted our own notions of "thinking" and assume their permanence, we forget how much human consciousness was restructured by the invention of writing.

4. Walter Benjamin, "The Work of Art in the Age of Mechanical Reproduction," in Hannah Arendt, ed., *Illuminations* (New York: Schocken Books, 1969), pp. 217–251.

5. Walter Benjamin, "A Small History of Photography," in *One-Way Street and Other Writings* (London: New Left Books, 1979), pp. 240–257.

6. Benjamin, *One-Way Street*, p. 91.

7. Quoted in Richard Wolin, *Walter Benjamin: An Aesthetic of Redemption* (New York: Columbia University Press, 1984), p. 130.

8. Aragon's book has reappeared in English as *Paris Peasant* (Boston: Exact Change, 1993).

9. Quoted in Wolin, *Walter Benjamin*, p. 128.

10. Rosalind E. Krauss, "The Photographic Conditions of Surrealism," in Krauss, ed., *The Originality of the Avant-Garde and Other Modernist Myths* (Cambridge, Mass.: MIT Press, 1985), pp. 103, 112–113.

11. Godard's famous line occurs in his second feature, *Le Petit Soldat* (1960).

12. Louis Aragon, "On Décor," in Paul Hammond, ed., *The Shadow and Its Shadow: Surrealist Writings on Cinema* (London: British Film Institute, 1978), p. 29. Compare Aragon's descriptions of the cinema's effect with Benjamin's famous remark that "not for nothing have Atget's photographs been likened to those of the scene of a

crime" ("A Small History of Photography," in *One-Way Street*, p. 256). Several of Hopper's most well-known paintings share this sinister quality. *Drug Store* (1927) and *Seven A.M.* (1948), for example, make their small shops seem vulnerable, as if a robbery, timed for these deserted times of day, were imminent. *Drug Store*, in fact, resembles the site of the surprise attack on *The Godfather's* Don Corleone. Similarly, *Cape Cod Evening* (1939) seems to portray a rural hideout, reached by the highway visible in *Gas* (1940). Meanwhile, the other gang members wait in a *Hotel by a Railroad* (1952), or in the *Hotel Lobby* (1943); or they meet surreptitiously with their accountant in a *Conference at Night* (1949). Indeed, in Hopper's world, even the smallest detail—ordinary curtains, blown by the wind (*Night Windows*, 1928)—becomes ominous.

13. Benjamin, "Surrealism: The Last Snapshot of the European Intelligentsia," in *One-Way Street*, p. 229.

14. Aragon, "On Décor," in *The Shadow and Its Shadow*, p. 29.

15. For a discussion of conventional cinema's narrative linearization, see Noël Burch, "Film's Institutional Mode of Representation and the Soviet Response," *October* 11 (Winter 1979): pp. 77–96.

16. André Breton, "As in a Wood," in *The Shadow and Its Shadow*, pp. 42–44.

17. Benjamin, "Surrealism," in *One-Way Street*, p. 229.

18. Quoted in Robert Hobbs, *Edward Hopper* (New York: Harry N. Abrams, 1987), pp. 10–11.

19. See *Roland Barthes* (New York: Hill and Wang, 1977), pp. 54–55: "*Le plein du cinéma*—Saturation of the cinema. Resistance to the cinema. The signifier itself is always, by nature, continuous here, whatever the rhetoric of frames and shots; without remission, a continuum of images; the film . . . *follows*, like a garrulous ribbon: statutory impossibility of the fragment, of the haiku."

20. Roland Barthes, "The Third Meaning," in *Image Music Text* (New York: Hill and Wang, 1977), pp. 52–68.

21. Barthes, "The Third Meaning," in *Image Music Text*, pp. 61–62.

22. Barthes, "The Third Meaning," in *Image Music Text*, pp. 64–65.

23. For a longer discussion of fetishism as a research strategy, see my book *The Avant-Garde Finds Andy Hardy* (Cambridge, Mass.: Harvard University Press, 1995), chap. 5.

24. Roland Barthes, "*Longtemps, je me suis couché de bonne heure . . .*," in *The Rustle of Language* (New York: Hill and Wang, 1986), pp. 278–279.

25. *Godard on Godard*, ed. Tom Milne (New York: Viking Press, 1972), p. 181: "Cinema, Truffaut said, is spectacle—Méliès—and research—Lumière. If I analyze myself today, I see that I have always wanted, basically, to do research in the form of a spectacle. The documentary side is: a man in a particular situation. The spectacle comes when one makes this man a gangster or a secret agent."

8. The Riddle of Elvis-the-Actor

1. David Thomson, *A Biographical Dictionary of Film*, 3rd ed. (New York: Alfred A. Knopf, 1994), p. 602.

2. John Lahr, "Sinatra's Song," *New Yorker*, 3 November 1997, p. 83. Lahr's *New Yorker* essay appears, in expanded form, as *Sinatra: The Artist and the Man* (New York: Random House, 1997). LaRosa's comment appeared in Gene Lees's tribute, "Turning a 32-Bar Song into a 3-Act Play," *New York Times*, 24 May 1998, Arts and Leisure section, p. 28.

3. Ronald L. Davis, *The Glamour Factory: Inside Hollywood's Big Studio System* (Dallas: Southern Methodist University Press, 1993), p. 113.

4. See James Naremore, *Acting in the Cinema* (Berkeley: University of California Press, 1988). This book has greatly influenced this essay.

5. Sinatra: "I always believed that the written word was first. Always first. The word actually dictates to you in a song. It really tells you what it needs" (Lahr, *Sinatra: The Artist and the Man*, p. 37).

6. See Naremore, *Acting in the Cinema*, pp. 17–19, for the notion of the-self-as-performance in *Breathless*.

9. The Two Cities and the Archive

1. Sigmund Freud, *The Origins of Psychoanalysis: Letters to Wilhelm Fliess*, trans. Eric Mosbacher and James Strachey (New York: Basic Books, 1954), p. 216.

2. Robert Scholes and Robert Kellogg, *The Nature of Narrative* (New York: Oxford University Press, 1966), pp. 13–15.

3. Roland Barthes, "The Reality Effect," in *The Rustle of Language*, trans. Richard Howard (New York: Hill and Wang, 1986), pp. 141–148.

4. Daniel Defoe, *Robinson Crusoe* (New York: Norton, 1975), p. 5.

5. Roland Barthes, "The Third Meaning," in *Image Music Text*, trans. Stephen Heath (New York: Hill and Wang, 1977), pp. 52–68.

6. Jorge Luis Borges, *Labyrinths* (New York: New Direction, 1964), p. 83.

7. Jean Baudrillard, *Selected Writings*, ed. Mark Poster (Stanford: Stanford University Press, 1988), pp. 125, 128.

8. Donald Spence, *Narrative Truth and Historical Truth: Meaning and Interpretation in Psychoanalysis* (New York: Norton, 1982), p. 32.

9. Jean-Luc Godard, *Godard on Godard*, ed. Tom Milne (New York: Viking, 1972), pp. 169, 181, 192, 235.

10. Quoted in Dudley Andrew, ed., *Breathless* (New Brunswick, N.J.: Rutgers University Press, 1987), p. 166.

11. Roland Barthes, *"Longtemps, je me suis couché de bonne heure . . . ,"* in *The Rustle of Language*, trans. Richard Howard (New York: Hill and Wang, 1986), pp. 278–279.

12. Bill Nichols, *Ideology and the Image* (Bloomington: Indiana University Press, 1981), p. 70.

13. The "Signorelli episode," Freud's account of his forgetting of that name and his attempts to replace it with the names of two other Italian Renaissance painters (Botticelli and Boltraffio) appears in the first chapter of *The Psychopathology of Everyday Life*, trans. Alan Tyson (New York: Norton, 1965), pp. 1–7.

14. Baudrillard, *Selected Writings*, p. 125.

15. Noël Burch, *Theory of Film Practice* (Princeton: Princeton University Press, 1981), pp. 111–112.

16. The best account of the *Cinémathèque Française* and its founder Henri Langlois is Richard Roud's book *A Passion for Films: Henri Langlois and the Cinémathèque Française* (New York: Viking, 1983).

10. Film and Literature

1. Walter J. Ong, *Interfaces of the Word: Studies in the Evolution of Consciousness and Culture* (Ithaca: Cornell University Press, 1977), p. 82.

2. Jacques Bontemps, Jean-Louis Comolli, Michael Delalaye, and Jean Narboni, "Struggle on Two Fronts: A Conversation with Jean-Luc Godard," *Film Quarterly* XXI, no. 2 (Winter 1968–1969): p. 31. A more complete version of Godard's famously cryptic remark: "When you get right down to it, the most fantastic thing you could film

is people reading. I don't see why no one's done it. Film someone who's simply reading. . . . The movie you'd make would be a lot more interesting than most of them are. Why couldn't film mean people reading really fine books? Why shouldn't you see something like that on TV, especially now that people don't read much?" Earlier in this same interview, Godard confesses, "You know I can't read" (25).

3. Louis D. Giannetti, *Godard and Others: Essays on Film Form* (Rutherford, N.J.: Fairleigh Dickinson University Press, 1975), p. 89.

4. George Bluestone, *Novels into Film: The Metamorphosis of Fiction into Cinema* (Berkeley: University of California Press, 1968); Robert Richardson, *Literature and Film* (Bloomington: Indiana University Press, 1969).

5. Richardson, *Literature and Film*, pp. 194–218. This chapter is discussed (critically) in James Goodwin, "Literature and Film: A Review of Criticism," *Quarterly Review of Film Studies* IV, no. 2 (Spring 1974): pp. 227–246 (see especially pp. 229–230). Goodwin's survey article provides the best early introduction to Film and Literature as a topic. By far the best recent survey is Timothy Corrigan's *Film and Literature: An Introduction and Reader* (Upper Saddle River, N.J.: Prentice-Hall, 1999).

6. The topic's main journal is *Literature/Film Quarterly*, begun in 1973 at Salisbury State College. Of the earlier books, Seymour Chatman's *Story and Discourse: Narrative Structure in Fiction and Film* (Ithaca: Cornell University Press, 1978) and Dudley Andrew's chapter "Adaptation," in *Concepts in Film Theory* (New York: Oxford University Press, 1984), seem the most abidingly useful.

7. I am using the word *apparatus* in Brecht's sense to mean the conditions under which information is produced, distributed, and consumed. As Brecht pointed out, in a justifiably famous remark, "Great apparati like the opera, the stage, the press, etc., impose their views as it were incognito" (*Brecht on Theatre*, ed. John Willett [New York: Hill and Wang, 1964], p. 34).

8. For an excellent discussion of this point, see Seymour Chatman, "What Novels Can Do that Films Can't (and Vice Versa)," *Critical Inquiry* 7, no. 1 (Autumn 1980): pp. 121–122. Robert Scholes makes the same point in *Semiotics and Interpretation* (New Haven: Yale University Press, 1982), p. 57.

9. Roland Barthes, *S/Z*, trans. Richard Miller (New York: Hill and Wang, 1974), p. 205.

10. For two excellent discussions of how the apparently extratextual (e.g., publicity, distribution, even rumor) inflects the readings of a particular text, see Tony Bennett, "Text and Social Process: The Case of James Bond," *Screen Education* 41 (Winter/Spring 1982): pp. 3–14; and Annette Kuhn, *Women's Pictures: Feminism and the Cinema* (London: Routledge and Kegan Paul, 1982), pp. 3–18, 125–126, 178–196.

11. I recognize that this point is debatable. A counterargument might invoke Barthes's *S/Z* as evidence of the radical intertextuality of all texts. But we often forget that *S/Z*'s point is based on an analysis of a *popular* text, Balzac's *Sarrasine*.

12. M. M. Bakhtin, *The Dialogic Imagination*, trans. Caryl Emerson and Michael Holquist (Austin: University of Texas, 1981), pp. 263, 428.

13. Roland Barthes, *Image Music Text*, trans. Stephen Heath (New York: Hill and Wang, 1977), pp. 32–51.

14. Judith Mayne, for example, superbly outlined *S/Z*'s importance to Film and Literature in "Introduction: Film/Narrative/The Novel," *Ciné-Tracts* 13 (1981): not paginated. I am also thinking here of Julia Lesage, who quickly saw *S/Z*'s relevance to film study. See her "*S/Z* and Film Criticism" and "*S/Z* and *Rules of the Game*," *Jump Cut* 12/13 (1976): pp. 41–51; and "Teaching the Comparative Analysis of Novels and Films," *Style* 9 (1975): pp. 453–468. Lesage studied in Indiana University's comparative literature program and cofounded *Jump Cut*.

15. Marshall McLuhan, *Understanding Media: The Extensions of Man* (New York: McGraw-Hill, 1964), p. vii.

16. Dudley Andrew, "The Well-Worn Muse: Adaptation in Film History and Theory," in *Narrative Strategies: Original Essays in Film and Prose Fiction*, ed. Syndy M. Conger and Janice R. Welsch (Macomb: Western Illinois University Press, 1980), p. 10. This estimate may be high. John Ellis says that "about 30 percent of all narrative films made in Hollywood's classic period were adapted from novels and short stories" ("The Literary Adaptation," *Screen* 23, no. 1 [May–June 1982]: p. 3). Even working from the other direction, the percentages still startle: the *New York Times* once estimated that one in fifty novels gets optioned for the movies (Edwin McDowell, "Hollywood and the Novelist: It's a Fickle Romance, at Best," *New York Times*, 14 July 1985, sec. 2, p. 1).

17. Between 1952 and 1955, all the major Hollywood studios (except MGM) sold most of their pre-1948 films to distributors who promptly sold them to local TV stations. See Erik Barnouw, *Tube of Plenty: The Evolution of American Television* (New York: Oxford University Press, 1975), pp. 197–198. By 1968, apart from its non-prime-time showings, television had an *NBC Monday Night Movie*, an *NBC Tuesday Night Movie*, an *ABC Wednesday Night Movie*, a *CBS Thursday Night Movie*, a *CBS Friday Night Movie*, an *NBC Saturday Night Movie*, and to complete the week, an *ABC Sunday Night Movie*. For listings of the annual prime-time schedules, see Tim Brooks and Earle Marsh, *The Complete Directory to Prime Time Network and Cable TV Shows 1946–Present* (New York: Ballantine, 1995).

18. Noël Burch, "Charles Baudelaire versus Doctor Frankenstein," *Afterimage* (London) 8/9 (Spring 1981): pp. 4–21.

19. For portions of Burch's argumentative archaeology of the cinema, see the following: "Porter, or Ambivalence," *Screen* 19, no. 4 (Winter 1978–1979): pp. 91–105; "Film's Institutional Mode of Representation and the Soviet Response," *October* 11 (Winter 1979): pp. 77–96; "A Parenthesis on Film History," in Burch's *To the Distant Observer: Form and Meaning in the Japanese Cinema* (Berkeley: University of California Press, 1979), pp. 61–66; and "How We Got into Pictures: Notes Accompanying *Correction Please*," *Afterimage* (London) 8/9 (Spring 1981): pp. 22–38. Burch summarized this argument in his book *Life to Those Shadows*, trans. Ben Brewster (Berkeley: University of California Press, 1990). The book, however, proved less interestingly provocative than the articles from which it derived.

Burch bases part of his argument about the "embourgeoisement" of the cinema on Russell Merritt's landmark article, "Nickelodeon Theaters, 1905–1914: Building an Audience for the Movies," in *The American Film Industry*, ed. Tino Balio (Madison: University of Wisconsin Press, 1985), pp. 83–102. Another excellent article in this tradition is Margaret Morse's "Paradoxes of Realism: The Rise of Film in the Train of the Novel," *Ciné-Tracts* 13 (Spring 1981): pp. 27–37.

20. Roland Barthes, *Writing Degree Zero*, trans. Annette Lavers and Colin Smith (New York: Hill and Wang, 1968).

21. Readers interested in a brief description of Classic Hollywood's stylistic protocols may wish to consult my book *A Certain Tendency of the Hollywood Cinema, 1930–1980* (Princeton: Princeton University Press, 1985), pp. 32–55.

22. "George Mitchell, "The Consolidation of the American Film Industry 1915–1920," *Ciné-Tracts* 6 (Spring 1979): pp. 28–36, and *Ciné-Tracts* 7/8 (Fall 1979): pp. 63–70.

23. In *S/Z*, Barthes wittily observes that often a narrative's sheer *speed* keeps a reader from asking questions (p. 127).

24. Another precedent was Arnold Hauser's monumental, four-volume *The Social History of Art* (New York: Vintage), which first appeared in the United States in 1951.

25. The leading book in this "constructivist" tradition is, of course, *S/Z*. A useful

summary of this position appears in Tony Stevens, "Reading the Realist Film," *Screen Education* 26 (Spring 1978): pp. 13–35. Other important discussions in this vein include Colin MacCabe, "Realism and the Cinema: Notes on Some Brechtian Theses," *Screen* 15, no. 2 (Summer 1974): pp. 7–27; Terry Lovell, *Pictures of Reality: Aesthetics, Politics and Pleasure* (London: British Film Institute, 1980); Sylvia Harvey, *May '68 and Film Culture* (London: British Film Institute, 1978); and Catherine Belsey, *Critical Practice* (London: Methuen, 1980).

26. Jeffrey Egan Welch, *Literature and Film: An Annotated Bibliography, 1909–1977* (New York: Garland, 1981).

27. Thomas Kuhn, *The Structure of Scientific Revolutions* (Chicago: University of Chicago Press, 1970), pp. 10–22, 43–51.

28. Quoted by Terence Hawkes in *Structuralism and Semiotics* (Berkeley: University of California Press, 1977), p. 152. Hawkes's book contains a useful summary of New Criticism's assumptions: pp. 151–156.

29. These words come from one of New Criticism's manifestos, W. K. Wimsatt and Monroe Beardsley's "The Intentional Fallacy," in Wimsatt, *The Verbal Icon: Studies in the Meaning of Poetry* (Lexington: University of Kentucky Press, 1954).

30. The title of Cleanth Brooks's famous essay, found in his book *The Well Wrought Urn: Studies in the Structure of Poetry* (New York: Harcourt, Brace & World, 1947), pp. 192–214.

31. An actual title of an article by William Fadiman who, in fact, criticized the tendency I am describing: *Films and Filming* 11, no. 5 (1965): pp. 21–23.

32. For film students, a convenient place to find Walter Benjamin's famous essay "The Work of Art in the Age of Mechanical Reproduction" is in *Film Theory and Criticism*, ed. Leo Braudy and Marshall Cohen (New York: Oxford University Press, 1999), pp. 731–751. It also appears, differently translated, in Benjamin's *Illuminations* (New York: Schocken, 1969).

33. Jacques Derrida, "Signature Event Context," *Glyph* 1 (1977): p. 185.

34. Derrida, in *Film Theory and Criticism*, pp. 733–734, 736.

35. *Critical Inquiry* 7, no. 1 (Autumn 1980): pp. 121–140.

36. Not surprisingly, initial work on television made the same mistake by simply carrying over a series of questions from film study that may or may not obtain in this different medium. When scholars trained in New Criticism's close-reading methods first approached the cinema, they inevitably gravitated to such apparently complex, ambiguous "art" films as Bergman's; and rightly so, since Hollywood films, while even more complex with their concealed reliance on intertextual networks, seemed slight in comparison. Making sense of how these popular movies worked required a whole new set of questions (having to do with ideology, semiotics, the experiences of reading and identification). Those issues may or may not apply to basic television genres. So far, the best work on television takes into account TV viewers' far more casual attention to images and sounds, which have become, for many people, part of the household furniture.

37. *The Bulletin of the Midwest Modern Language Association* 4, no. 1 (Spring 1971).

38. See, for example, Brian McCrea's argument that English professors' need for apparently complex texts has resulted in the banishment from the curriculum of the relatively straightforward Addison and Steele: *Addison and Steele Are Dead: The English Department, Its Canon, and the Professionalization of Literary Criticism* (Newark: University of Delaware Press, 1990). The most comprehensive discussion of how academic structures affect assumed notions about "Literature" and teaching appears in Gerald Graff, *Professing Literature: An Institutional History* (Chicago: University of Chicago Press, 1987). Also useful is Robert Scholes, *The Rise and Fall of English* (New Haven: Yale University Press, 1998).

39. Jonathan Culler, "The Critical Assumption," *SCE Reports* 6 (Fall 1979) (The Society for Critical Exchange), p. 83.

40. I have written elsewhere about the job market's pernicious effect on the *kinds* of film studies work that gets published: see my book *The Avant-Garde Finds Andy Hardy* (Cambridge, Mass: Harvard University Press, 1995), pp. 5–10.

41. C. Carr, "M. Kasper's Glyph Hangers," *The Village Voice Literary Supplement*, March 1985, p. 19.

42. Andrew, "The Well-Worn Muse: Adaptation in Film History and Theory," pp. 12–13. For an excellent discussion of "the discourse of fidelity," see Christopher Orr, "The Discourse on Adaptation," *Wide Angle* 6, no. 2 (1984): pp. 72–76.

43. On Freud's analogy of the unconscious and the dream to the rebus, see *The Interpretation of Dreams*, trans. A. A. Brill (New York: Modern Library, 1950).

On the ideogram, see Sergei Eisenstein, "The Cinematographic Principle and the Ideogram," in his *Film Form*, trans. Jay Leyda (New York: Harcourt, 1949), pp. 28–44; and Ernest Fenollosa, *The Chinese Written Character as a Medium for Poetry*, ed. Ezra Pound (San Francisco: City Lights Books, 1936).

For Barthes's semiotic investigations, see "The Photographic Message" and "Rhetoric of the Image," in his *Image Music Text*, trans. Stephen Heath (New York: Hill and Wang, 1977), pp. 7–31.

Almost all of Godard's films explore the relationship between word and image (he calls his own production company *Sonimage*). I am thinking in particular of two scenes: the first, in *Masculin-Féminin* (1966), where the image of the pretty "Mademoiselle 19 Ans" competes with the tendentious caption ("Dialogue with a Consumer Product") that introduces her; the second, in *2 ou 3 choses que je sais d'elle* (1966), where consecutive voiceovers introduce the same woman as first actress and then fictional character.

The best article on Eikhenbaum's "inner speech" is Paul Willemen's "Cinematic Discourse: The Problem of Inner Speech," in his *Looks and Frictions: Essays in Cultural Studies and Film Theory* (Bloomington: Indiana University Press/British Film Institute, 1994), pp. 27–55. See also my book *The Avant-Garde Finds Andy Hardy* (Cambridge, Mass.: Harvard University Press, 1995), chap. 2.

On renaissance memory systems, see Frances Yates, *The Art of Memory* (Chicago: University of Chicago Press, 1966). For a fascinating historical extrapolation from Yates's work, see Jonathan D. Spence, *The Memory Palace of Matteo Ricci* (New York: Viking, 1984).

The best study of Derrida's interest in hieroglyphics is Gregory L. Ulmer's *Applied Grammatology: Post(e)-Pedagogy from Jacques Derrida to Joseph Beuys* (Baltimore: Johns Hopkins University Press, 1985).

On the *caméra-stylo*, see Alexandre Astruc, "*Le caméra-stylo*," in *The New Wave*, ed. Peter Graham (Garden City, N.Y.: Doubleday, 1968), pp. 17–24.

44. See Havelock's *Preface to Plato* (Cambridge, Mass.: Harvard University Press, 1963) and *The Literate Revolution in Greece and Its Cultural Consequences* (Princeton: Princeton University Press, 1982).

45. Hauser, *The Social History of Art*, vol. 4 (New York: Vintage, 1951), pp. 226–259.

I N D E X

Page numbers in *italics* refer to illustrations.

Robert B. Ray, Director of Film and Media Studies and Professor of English at the University of Florida, is author of *A Certain Tendency of the Hollywood Cinema 1930–1980* and *The Avant-Garde Finds Andy Hardy*. He is also a member of The Vulgar Boatmen, whose records include *You and Your Sister, Please Panic,* and *Opposite Sex*.